*To
Remember
Spain*

To Remember Spain

The Anarchist and Syndicalist Revolution of 1936

Essays by
Murray Bookchin

Library of Congress Cataloguing-in-Publication Data

Bookchin, Murray, 1921-
    To Remember Spain: The Anarchist and Syndicalist
Revolution of 1936 / essays by Murray Bookchin,
        p.   cm.
    ISBN 1-873176-87 2 : $4.50
    1. Spain--History--Civil War, 1938-1939. 2. Anarchism--
Spain--History--20th century. 3. Syndicalism--Spain--History
--20th century. I. Title.

DP269.B658 1994

946.081--dc20   94-13760
                                                            CIP

British Library Cataloguing in Publication Data

    A catalogue record for this title is available from the
    British Library.

First published in 1994 by
    AK Press   AK Press
    22 Lutton Place   P.O. Box 40682
    Edinburgh, Scotland   San Francisco, CA
    EH8 9PE   94140-0682

The publication of this book was in part, made possible by the
generosity of the **Friends of AK Press**, with particular thanks to
Joe Williams.

*Typeset and design donated by Freddie Baer. Illustrations by Sim,
from Estampas de la Revolución Española 19 Julio de 1936.*

Contents

Preface 1

An Overview of the Spanish Libertarian Movement 3

After Fifty Years: The Spanish Civil War 40

Preface

These essays are less an analysis of the Spanish Revolution and Civil War of 1936-39 than an evocation of the greatest proletarian and peasant revolution to occur over the past two centuries. Although they contain a general overview and evaluation of the Anarchist and Anarchosyndicalist movements (the two should be clearly distinguished) in the three-year struggle at the end of the 1930s, they are not intended to be a full account of those complex events.

It is no exaggeration to say that the Spanish Revolution was the farthest-reaching movement that the Left ever produced, for reasons the essays that follow will make clear. The Spanish proletariat and peasantry, led largely by Anarchist militants whose names will never be known to us, strained the limits of what we in the 1930s called "proletarian socialism" and went appreciably beyond them. Far more than the leaders of the Anarchosyndicalist National Confederation of Labor and the Iberian Anarchist Federation (CNT-FAI) expected or apparently even wanted, Anarchists and Anarchosyndicalists spontaneously formed the famous industrial and agrarian collectives that so markedly distinguished the Spanish Revolution from any that had preceded it. They provided the militiamen and women who died by the thousands in the early fighting against the Francoist generals who led the military uprising of July 1936 in behalf of the Spanish landlords, the industrial bourgeoisie, and the Church.

The endeavors of the Anarchists and their Left Socialist allies in the Spanish Revolution must never be forgotten, lest today's Left lose a sense of continuity with the revolutionary era — its idealism, principles, and ideas. The loss of this continuity would contribute to political opportunism and to a fashionable ideological pluralism that mingles reformist politics with radical rhetoric as the need arises.

The essays that follow attempt to reach a wider readership than do the more academic studies of the events. The first essay, retitled here "An Overview of the Spanish Libertarian Movement," consists of my September 1973 introductory essay to Sam Dolgoff's *The Anarchist Collectives: Workers' Self-Management in the Spanish Revolution 1936-1939* (New York: Free Life Editions, 1974), which was more of a compendium of excerpts than a comprehensive work in its own right. The second essay, "After Fifty Years: The Spanish Civil War," published in *New Politics*, n.s., vol. 1, no. 1 (Summer 1986), was written to commemorate the half-century anniversary of the Spanish Revolution.* I wish to thank my friends Phyllis and Julius Jacobson, the editors of *New Politics*, for their kind permission to reprint the essay here.

I dedicate this book to the CNT-FAI revolutionaries Gastón Leval and José Peirats — two astonishingly honest and committed comrades.

Murray Bookchin
Institute for Social Ecology
Plainfield Vermont 05667
February 28, 1993

---

* *New Politics*, P.O. Box 98, Brooklyn, New York 11231.

An Overview
of the Spanish Libertarian Movement

In the morning hours of July 18, 1936, General Francisco Franco issued the *pronunciamiento* from Las Palmas in Spanish North Africa that openly launched the struggle of Spain's reactionary military officers against the legally elected Popular Front government in Madrid.

The Franco *pronunciamiento* left little doubt that, in the event of victory by the Spanish generals, the parliamentary republic would be replaced by a clearly authoritarian state, modeled institutionally on similar regimes in Germany and Italy. The Francoist forces or "Nationalists," as they were to call themselves, exhibited all the trappings and ideologies of the fascist movements of the day: the raised open-palm salute, the appeals to a "folk-soil" philosophy of order, duty, and obedience, and the avowed commitments to smash the labor movement and end all political dissidence. To the world, the conflict initiated by the Spanish generals seemed like another of the classic struggles waged between the "forces of fascism" and the "forces of democracy" that reached such acute proportions in the thirties. What distinguished the Spanish conflict from similar struggles in Italy, Germany, and Austria, however, was the massive resistance with which the "forces of democracy" seemed to oppose to the Spanish military. Franco and his military co-conspirators, despite the wide support they enjoyed among the officer cadres in the army, grossly miscalculated the popular opposition they would encounter. The so-called "Spanish Civil War" lasted nearly three years — from July 1936 to March 1939 — and claimed an estimated million lives.

For the first time, so it seemed to many of us in the thirties, an entire people with dazzling courage had arrested the terrifying success of fascist movements in central and southern Europe. Scarcely three years earlier, Hitler had pocketed Germany without a shred of resistance from the massive Marxist-dominated German labor movement. Austria, two years before, had succumbed to an essentially authoritarian state after a week of futile street-fighting by Socialist workers in Vienna. Everywhere fascism seemed "on the march" and "democracy" in retreat. But Spain had seriously resisted — and continued to resist for years despite the armaments, aircraft, and troops which Franco acquired from Italy and Germany. To radicals and liberals alike, the Spanish Civil War was being waged not only on the Iberian Peninsula but in every country where "democracy" seemed threatened by the rising tide of domestic and international fascist movements. The Spanish Civil War, we were led to believe, was a struggle between a liberal republic that was valiantly and with popular support trying to defend a democratic parliamentary state against authoritarian generals — an imagery that is conveyed to this very day by most books on the subject and by that shabby cinematic documentary *To Die in Madrid*.

What so few of us knew outside Spain, however, was that the Spanish Civil War was in fact a sweeping social revolution by millions of workers and peasants who were concerned not to rescue a treacherous republican regime but to reconstruct Spanish society along revolutionary lines. We would scarcely have learned from the press that these workers and peasants viewed the Republic almost with as much animosity as they did the Francoists. Indeed, acting largely on their own initiative against "republican" ministers who were trying to betray them to the generals, they had raided arsenals and sporting-goods stores for weapons and with incredible valor had aborted military conspiracies in most of the cities and towns of Spain. We were almost totally oblivious to the fact that these workers and peasants had seized and collectivized most of the factories and land in republican-held areas, establishing a new social order based on direct control of the country's productive resources by workers' committees and peasant assemblies. While the republic's institutions lay in debris, abandoned by most of its military and police forces, the workers and peasants had created their own institutions to administer the cities in Republican Spain, formed their own armed workers' squads to patrol the streets, and established a remarkable revolutionary militia force with which to fight the Francoist forces — a voluntaristic militia in which men and women elected their own commanders and in which military rank conferred no social, material, or symbolic distinctions. Largely unknown to us at that time, the Spanish workers and peasants had made a sweeping social revolution. They had created their own revolutionary social forms to administer the country as well as to wage war against a well-trained and well-supplied army. The "Spanish Civil War" was not a political conflict between a liberal democracy and a fascist military corps but a deeply socio-economic conflict between the workers and peasants of Spain and their historic class enemies, ranging from the landowning grandees and clerical overlords inherited from the past to the rising industrial bourgeoisie and bankers of more recent times.

The revolutionary scope of this conflict was concealed from us — by "us" I refer to the many thousands of largely Communist-influenced radicals of the "red" thirties who responded to the struggle in Spain with the same fervor and agony that young people of the sixties responded to the struggle in Indochina. We need not turn to Orwell or Borkenau, radicals of obviously strong anti-Stalinist convictions, for an explanation of this fervor. Burnett Bolloten, a rather politically innocent United Press reporter who happened to be stationed in Madrid at the time, conveys his own sense of moral outrage at the misrepresentation of the Spanish conflict in the opening lines of his superbly documented study, *The Grand Camouflage:*

> Although the outbreak of the Spanish Civil War in July, 1936, was followed by a far-reaching social-revolution in the anti-Franco camp — more profound in some respects than the Bolshevik Revolution in its early stages — millions of discerning people outside of Spain were kept in ignorance, not only of its depth and range, but even of its existence, by virtue of a policy of duplicity and dissimulation of which there is no parallel in history.

Foremost in practicing this deception upon the world, and in misrepresenting in Spain itself the character of the revolution, were the Communists, who, although but an exiguous minority when the Civil War began, used so effectually the manifold opportunities which that very upheaval presented that before the close of the conflict in 1939 they became, behind a democratic frontispiece, the ruling force in the left camp.

The details of this deception could fill several large volumes. The silence that gathers around Spain, like a bad conscience, attests to the fact that the events are very much alive — as are the efforts to misrepresent them. After nearly forty years the wounds have not healed. In fact, as the recent revival of Stalinism suggests, the disease that produced the purulence of counterrevolution in Spain still lingers on in the American left. But to deal with the Stalinist counterrevolution in Spain is beyond the scope of these remarks. It might be useful, however, to examine the revolutionary tendencies that unfolded prior to July 1936 and explore the influence they exercised on the Spanish working class and peasantry. Their collectives were not the results of virginal popular spontaneity, important as popular spontaneity was, nor were they nourished exclusively by the collectivist legacy of traditional Spanish village society. Revolutionary ideas and movements played a crucial role of their own and their influence deserves the closest examination.

The Spanish generals started a military rebellion in July 1936; the Spanish workers and peasants answered them with a social revolution — and this revolution was largely anarchist in character. I say this provocatively even though the Socialist UGT was numerically as large as the anarchosyndicalist CNT.[1] During the first few months of the military rebellion, Socialist workers in Madrid often acted as radically as anarchosyndicalist workers in Barcelona. They established their own militias, formed street patrols, and expropriated a number of strategic factories, placing them under the control of workers' committees. Similarly, Socialist peasants in Castile and Estramadura formed collectives, many of which were as libertarian as those created by anarchist peasants in Aragon and the Levant. In the opening "anarchic" phase of the revolution, so similar to the opening phases of earlier revolutions, the "masses" tried to assume direct control over society and exhibited a remarkable élan in improvising their own libertarian forms of social administration.

Looking back beyond this opening phase, however, it is fair to say that the durability of the collectives in Spain, their social scope, and the resistance they offered to the Stalinist counter-revolution, depended largely on the extent to which they were under anarchist influence. What distinguishes the Spanish Revolution from those which preceded it is not only the fact that it placed much of Spain's economy in the hands of workers' committees and peasant assemblies or that it established a democratically elected militia system. These social forms, in varying degrees, had emerged during the Paris Commune and in the early period of the Russian Revolution. What made the Spanish Revolution unique was its workers' control and collectives which had been advocated for nearly three generations by a massive libertarian movement and which became one of the most serious issues to divide the so-called "republican" camp (together with the fate of the militia system). Owing to the scope of its libertarian social forms, not only did the Spanish Revolution prove to be "more profound" (to borrow Bolloten's phrase) than the Bolshevik Revolution, but the influence of a deeply rooted anarchist ideology and the intrepidity of anarchist militants virtually produced a civil war within the civil war.

Indeed, in many respects, the revolution of 1936 marked the culmination of more than sixty years of anarchist agitation and activity in Spain. To understand this, we must go back to the early 1870s, when the Italian anarchist Giuseppi Fanelli introduced Bakunin's ideas to groups of workers and intellectuals in Madrid and Barcelona. Fanelli's encounter with young workers of the *Fomento de las Artes* in Madrid, a story told with great relish by Gerald Brenan is almost legendary: the volatile speech that the tall bearded Italian anarchist who hardly knew a word of Spanish delivered to a small but enthusiastic audience that scarcely understood his free-wheeling mixture of French and Italian. By dint of sheer mimicry, tonal inflections, and a generous

To Remember Spain

use of cognates, Fanelli managed to convey enough of Bakunin's ideals to gain the group's adherence and to establish the founding Spanish section of the International Working Men's Association or so-called "First International." Thereafter, the "Internationalists," as the early Spanish anarchists were known, expanded rapidly from their circles in Madrid and Barcelona to Spain as a whole, taking strong root especially in Catalonia and Andalusia. Following the definitive split between the Marxists and Bakuninists at the Hague Congress of the IWMA in September 1872, the Spanish section remained predominantly Bakuninist in its general outlook. Marxism did not become a significant movement in Spain until the turn of the century, and even after it became an appreciable force in the labor movement, it remained largely reformist until well into the thirties. During much of its early history, the strength of the Spanish Socialist Party and the UGT lay in administrative areas such as Madrid rather than in predominantly working-class cities like Barcelona.[2] Marxism tended to appeal to the highly skilled, pragmatic, rather authoritarian Castilian; anarchism, to the unskilled, idealistic Catalans and the independent, liberty-loving mountain villagers of Andalusia and the Levant. The great rural masses of Andalusian day-workers or *braceros*, who remain to this day among the most oppressed and impoverished strata of European society, tended to follow the anarchists. But their allegiances varied with the fortunes of the day. In periods of upheaval, they swelled the ranks of the Bakuninist IWMA and its successor organizations in Spain, only to leave it in equally large numbers in periods of reaction.

Yet however much the fortunes of Spanish anarchism varied from region to region and from period to period, whatever revolutionary movement existed in Spain during this sixty-year period was essentially anarchist. Even as anarchism began to ebb before Marxian social-democratic and later Bolshevik organizations after the First World War, Spanish anarchism retained its enormous influence and its revolutionary élan. Viewed from a radical standpoint, the history of the Spanish labor movement remained libertarian and often served to define the contours of the Marxist movements in Spain. "Generally speaking, a small but well-organized group of Anarchists in a Socialist area drove the Socialists to the Left," observes Brenan, "whereas in predominantly Anarchist areas, Socialists were outstandingly reformist." It was not socialism but rather anarchism that determined the metabolism of the Spanish labor movement — the great general strikes that swept repeatedly over Spain, the recurring insurrections in Barcelona and in the towns and villages of Andalusia, and the gun battles between labor militants and employer-hired thugs in the Mediterranean coastal cities.

It is essential to emphasize that Spanish anarchism was not merely a program embedded in a dense theoretical matrix. It was a way of life: partly the life of the Spanish people as it was lived in the closely knit villages of the countryside and the intense neighborhood life of the working class barrios; partly, too, the theoretical articulation of that life as projected by Bakunin's concepts of decentralization, mutual aid, and popular organs of self-management. That Spain had a long tradition of agrarian collectivism is discussed in this book and examined in some detail in Joaquin Costa's *Colectivismo Agrario en Espagna*. Inasmuch as this tradition was distinctly precapitalist, Spanish Marxism regarded it as anachronistic, in fact as "historically reactionary." Spanish socialism built its agrarian program around the Marxist tenet that the peasantry and its social forms could have no lasting revolutionary value until they were "proletarianized" and "industrialized." Indeed, the sooner the village decayed the better, and the more rapidly the peasantry became a hereditary proletariat, "disciplined, united, organized by the very mechanism of the process of capitalist production itself" (Marx) — a distinctly hierarchical and authoritarian "mechanism" — the more rapidly Spain would advance to the tasks of socialism.

Spanish anarchism, by contrast, followed a decisively different approach. It sought out the precapitalist collectivist traditions of the village, nourished what was living and vital in them, evoked their revolutionary potentialities as liberatory modes of mutual aid and self-management, and deployed them to vitiate the obedience, hierarchical mentality, and authoritarian outlook fostered by the factory system. Ever mindful of the "embourgeoisment" of the proletariat (a term continually on Bakunin's lips in the later years of his life), the Spanish anarchists tried to use the precapitalist traditions of the a peasantry and working class against the assimilation of the workers' outlook to an authoritarian industrial rationality. In this respect, their efforts were favored by the continuous fertilization of the Spanish proletariat by rural workers who renewed these traditions daily as they migrated to the cities. The revolutionary élan of the Barcelona proletariat — like that of the Petrograd and Parisian proletariats — was due in no small measure to the fact that these workers never solidly sedimented into a hereditary working class, totally removed from precapitalist traditions, whether of the peasant or the craftsman. Along the Mediterranean coastal cities of Spain, many workers retained a living memory of a noncapitalist culture — one in which each moment of life was not strictly regulated by the punch clock, the factory whistle, the foreman, the machine, the highly regulated work day, and the atomizing world of the large city. Spanish anarchism flourished within a tension created by these antagonistic traditions and sensibilities. Indeed, where a "Germanic proletariat" (to use another of Bakunin's cutting phrases) emerged in Spain, it drifted either toward the UGT or toward the Catholic unions. Its political outlook, reformist when not overtly conservative, often clashed with the more *déclassé* working class of Catalonia and the Mediterranean coast, leading to conflicting tendencies within the Spanish proletariat as a whole.

Ultimately, in my view, the destiny of Spanish anarchism depended upon its ability to create libertarian organizational forms that could synthesize as the precapitalist collectivist traditions of the village with an industrial economy and a highly urbanized society. I speak here of no mere programmatic "alliance" between the Spanish peasantry and proletariat but more organically, of new organizational forms and sensibilities that imparted a revolutionary libertarian character to two social classes who lived in conflicting cultures. That Spain required a well-organized libertarian movement was hardly a matter of doubt among the majority of Spanish anarchists. But would this movement reflect a village society or a factory society? Where a conflict existed, could the two be melded in the same movement without violating the libertarian tenets of decentralization, mutual aid, and self-administration? In the classical era of "proletarian socialism" between 1848 and 1939, an era that stressed the "hegemony" of the industrial proletariat in all social struggles, Spanish anarchism followed a historic trajectory that revealed at once the limitations of the era itself and the creative possibilities for anarchic forms of organization.

By comparison with the cities, the Spanish villages that were committed to anarchism raised very few organizational problems. Brenan's emphasis on the *braceros* notwithstanding, the strength of agrarian anarchism in the south and the Levant lay in the mountain villages, not among the rural proletariat that worked the great plantations of Andalusia. In these relatively isolated villages, a fierce sense of independence and personal dignity whetted the bitter social hatreds engendered by poverty, creating the rural "patriarchs" of anarchism whose entire families were devoted almost apostolically to "the Idea." For these sharply etched and rigorously ascetic individuals, defiance of the State, the Church, and conventional authority in general was almost a way of life. Knitted together by the local press — and at various times there were hundreds of anarchist periodicals in Spain — they formed the sinews of agrarian anarchism from the 1870s onwards and, to a large extent, the moral conscience of Spanish anarchism throughout its history.

Their agrarian collectives reflected to a remarkable extent the organizational forms which the anarchists fostered among all the villages under their influence before the 1936 revolution. The revolution in rural communities essentially enlarged the old IWMA and later CNT nuclei, membership groups, or quite simply clans of closely knit anarchist families into popular assemblies. These usually met weekly and formulated the policy decisions of the community as a whole. The assembly form comprised the organizational ideal of village anarchism from the days of the first truly Bakuninist congress of the Spanish IWMA in Córdoba in 1872, stressing the libertarian traditions of Spanish village life.[3] Where such popular assemblies were possible, their decisions were executed by a committee elected from the assembly. Apparently, the right to recall committee members was taken for granted and they certainly enjoyed no privileges, emoluments, or institutional power. Their influence was a function of their obvious dedication and capabilities. It remained a cardinal principle of Spanish anarchists never to pay their delegates, even when the CNT numbered a million members.[4] Normally, the responsibilities of elected delegates had to be discharged after working hours. Almost all the evenings of anarchist militants were occupied with meetings of one sort or another. Whether at assemblies or committees, they argued, debated, voted, and administered, and when time afforded, they read and passionately discussed "the Idea" to which they dedicated not only their leisure hours but their very lives. For the greater part of the day, they were working men and women, *obrera consciente*, who abjured smoking and drinking, avoided brothels and the bloody bull ring, purged their talk of "foul" language, and by their probity, dignity, respect for knowledge, and militancy tried to set a moral example for their entire class. They never used the word "god" in their daily conversations (*salud* was preferred over *adios*) and avoided all official contact with clerical and state authorities, indeed, to the point where they refused to legally validate their lifelong "free unions" with marital documents and never baptized or confirmed their children. One must know Catholic Spain to realize how far-reaching were these self-imposed mores — and how quixotically consistent some of them were with the puritanical traditions of the country.[5]

It is appropriate to note at this point that the myth, widely disseminated by the current sociological literature on the subject, that agrarian anarchism in Spain was antitechnological in spirit and atavistically sought to restore a neolithic "Golden Age" can be quite effectively refuted by a close study of the unique educational role played by the anarchists. Indeed, it was the anarchists, with inexpensive, simply written brochures, who brought the French enlightenment and modern scientific theory to the peasantry, not the arrogant liberals or the disdainful Socialists. Together with pamphlets on Bakunin and Kropotkin, the anarchist press published simple accounts of the theories of natural and social evolution and elementary introductions to the secular culture of Europe. They tried to instruct the peasants in advanced techniques of land management and earnestly favored the use of agricultural machinery to lighten the burdens of toil and provide more leisure for self-development. Far from being an atavistic trend in Spanish society, as Hobsbawm (in his

Primitive Rebels) and even Brenan would have us believe, I can say with certainty from a careful review of the issue that anarchism more closely approximated a radical popular enlightenment.

In their personal qualities, dedicated urban anarchists were not substantially different from their rural comrades. But in the towns and cities of Spain, these urban anarchists faced more difficult organizational problems. Their efforts to create libertarian forms of organization were favored, of course, by the fact that many Spanish workers were either former villagers or were only a generation or so removed from the countryside.[6] Yet the prospect for libertarian organization in the cities and factories could not depend upon the long tradition of village collectivism — the strong sense of community—that existed in rural anarchist areas. For within the factory itself — the realm of toil, hierarchy, industrial discipline, and brute material necessity—"community" was more a function of the bourgeois division of labor with its exploitative, even competitive connotations, than of humanistic cooperation, playfully creative work, and mutual aid. Working-class solidarity depended less upon a shared meaningful life nourished by self-fulfilling work than the common enemy — the boss — who exploded any illusion that under capitalism the worker was more than an industrial resource, an object to be coldly manipulated and ruthlessly exploited. If anarchism can be partly regarded as a revolt of the individual against the industrial system, the profound truth that lies at the heart of that revolt is that the factory routine not only blunts the sensibility of the worker to the rich feast of life; it degrades the worker's image of his or her human potentialities, of his or her capacities to take direct control of the means for administering social life.

One of the unique virtues that distinguished the Spanish anarchists from socialists was their attempt to *transform* the factory domain itself — a transformation that was to be effected in the long run by their demand for workers' self-management of production, and more immediately, by their attempt to form libertarian organizations that culminated in the formation of the syndicalist CNT. However, the extent to which workers' self-management can actually *eliminate* alienated labor and *alter* the impact of the factory system on the worker's sensibilities requires, in my view, a more probing analysis than it has hitherto received. The problem of the impact of the factory system on workers became crucial as the proletarian element in the CNT grew, while the anarchists sought to develop characteristics of initiative and self-management that were directly opposed to the characteristics inculcated by the factory system.

No sizable radical movement in modern times had seriously asked itself if organizational forms had to be developed which promoted changes in the most fundamental behavior patterns of its members. How could the libertarian movement vitiate the spirit of obedience, of hierarchical organization, of leader-and-led relationships, of authority and command instilled by capitalist industry? It is to the lasting credit of Spanish anarchism — and of anarchism generally — that it posed this question.[7] The term "integral personality" appears repeatedly in Spanish anarchist documents and tireless efforts were made to develop individuals who not only cerebrally accepted libertarian principles but tried to practice them. Accordingly, the organizational framework of the movement (as expressed in the IWMA, the CNT, and the FAI) was meant to be decentralized, to allow for the greatest degree of initiative and decision-making at the base, and to provide structural guarantees against the formation of a bureaucracy. These requirements, on the other hand, had to be balanced against the need for coordination, mobilized common action, and effective planning. The organizational history of anarchism in the cities and towns of Spain — the forms the anarchists created and those which they discarded — is largely an account of the pull between these two requirements and the extent to which one prevailed over the other. This tension was not merely a matter of experience and structural improvisation. In the long run, the outcome of the pull between decentralization and coordination depended on the ability of the most dedicated anarchists to affect the consciousness of the workers who entered anarchist influenced unions — specifically unions of a syndicalist character whose aims were not only to fight for immediate material gains but also to provide the infrastructure for a libertarian society.

Long before syndicalism became a popular term in the French labor movement of the late 1890s, it already existed in the early Spanish labor movement. The anarchist influenced Spanish Federation of the old IWMA, in my opinion, was distinctly syndicalist.

At the founding congress of the Spanish Federation at Barcelona in June 1870, the "commission on the theme of the social organization of the workers" proposed a structure that would form a model for all later anarchosyndicalist labor unions in Spain, including the CNT. The commission suggested a typical syndicalist dual structure: organization by trade and organization by locality. Local trade organizations (*Secciones de oficio*) grouped together all workers from a common enterprise and vocation into large occupational federations (*Uniones de oficio*) whose primary function was to struggle around economic grievances and working conditions. A local organization of a miscellaneous trades gathered up all those workers from different vocations whose numbers were too small to constitute effective organizations along vocational lines. Paralleling these vocational organizations, in every community and region where the IWMA was represented, the different local *Secciones* were grouped together, irrespective of trade, into local geographic bodies (*Federaciones locales*) whose function was avowedly revolutionary — the administration of social and economic life on a decentralized libertarian basis.

This dual structure forms the bedrock of all syndicalist forms of organization. In Spain, as elsewhere, the structure was knitted together by workers' committees, which originated in individual shops, factories, and agricultural communities. Gathering together in assemblies, the workers elected from their midst the committees that presided over the affairs of the vocational *Secciones de oficio* and the geographic *Federaciones locales*. They were federated into regional committees for nearly every large area of Spain. Every year, when possible, the workers elected the delegates to the annual congresses of the Spanish Federation of the IWMA, which in turn elected a national Federal Council. With the decline of the IWMA, syndicalist union federations surfaced and disappeared in different regions of Spain, especially Catalonia and Andalusia. The first was the rather considerable Workers' Federation of the 1880s. Following its suppression, Spanish anarchism contracted either to nonunion ideological groups such as the Anarchist Organization of the Spanish Region or to essentially regional union federations like the Catalan-based Pact of Union and Solidarity of the 1890s and Workers'

Solidarity of the early 1900s. Except for the short-lived Federation of Workers' Societies of the Spanish Region, established in 1900 on the initiative of a Madrid bricklayers' union, no major national syndicalist federation appeared in Spain until the organization of the CNT in 1911. With the establishment of the CNT, Spanish syndicalism entered its most mature and decisive period. Considerably larger than its rival, the UGT, the CNT became the essential arena for anarchist agitation in Spain.

The CNT was not merely "founded"; it developed organically out of the Catalan Workers' Solidarity and its most consolidated regional federation, the Catalan federation (*Confederación Regional del Trabajo de Cataluña.*) Later, other regional federations were established from local unions in each province — many of them lingering on from the Federation of Workers' Societies of the Spanish Region — until there were eight by the early 1930s. The national organization, in effect, was a loose collection of regional federations which were broken down into local and district federations and finally into *sindicatos*, or individual unions. These *sindicatos* (earlier, they were known by the dramatic name of *sociedades de resistencia al capital* — resistance societies to capital) were established on a vocational basis and, in typical syndicalist fashion, grouped into geographic and trade federations *(federaciones locales* and *sindicatos de oficio).* To coordinate this structure, the annual congresses of the CNT elected a National Committee which was expected to occupy itself primarily with correspondence, the collection of statistics, and aid to prisoners.

The statutes of the Catalan regional federation provide us with the guidelines used for the national movement as a whole. According to these statutes, the organization was committed to "direct action," rejecting all "political and religious interference." Affiliated district and local federations were to be "governed by the greatest autonomy possible, it being understood by this that they have complete freedom in all the professional matters relating to the individual trades which integrate them." Each member was expected to pay monthly dues of ten centimes (a trifling sum) which was to be divided equally among the local organization, the Regional Confederation, the National Confederation, the union newspaper (*Solidaridad Obrera* — "Workers' Solidarity"), and the all-important special fund for "social prisoners."

To Remember Spain

By statute, the Regional Committee — the regional equiva-
lent of the CNT's National Committee — was expected to be
merely an administrative body. Although it clearly played a
directive role in coordinating action, its activities were bound by
policies established by the annual regional congress. In unusual
situations, the Committee could consult local bodies, either by
referendums or by written queries. In addition to the annual
regional congresses at which the Regional Committee was elected,
the Committee was obliged to call extraordinary congresses at
the request of the majority of the local federations. The local
federations, in turn, were given three months' notice before a
regular congress so that they could "prepare the themes for
discussion." Within a month before the congress, the Regional
Committee was required to publish the submitted "themes" in
the union newspaper, leaving sufficient time for the workers to
define their attitudes toward the topics to be discussed and
instruct their delegates accordingly. The delegations to the
congress, whose voting power was determined by the number of
members they represented, were elected by general assemblies
of workers convened by the local and district federations.

These statutes formed the basis for the CNT's practice up to
the revolution of 1936. Although they notably lacked any provi-
sion for the recall of the committee members, the organization in
its heroic period was more democratic than the statutes would
seem to indicate. A throbbing vitality existed at the base of this
immense organization, marked by active interest in the CNT's
problems and considerable individual initiative. The workers'
centers (centros obreros), which the anarchists had established in
the days of the IWMA, were not only the local offices of the
union; they were also meeting places and cultural centers where
members went to exchange ideas and attend lectures. All the
affairs of the local CNT were managed by committees of ordi-
nary unpaid workers. Although the official union meetings were
held only once in three months, there were "conferences of an
instructive character" every Saturday night and Sunday
afternoon. The solidarity of the sindicatos was so intense that it
was not always possible to maintain an isolated strike. There was
always a tendency for a strike to trigger off others in its support
and generate active aid by other sindicatos.

In any case, this is the way the CNT tried to carry on its affairs and during favorable periods actually functioned. But there were periods when repression and sudden, often crucial, turns in events made it necessary to suspend annual or regional congresses and confine important policy-making decisions to plenums of leading committees or to "congresses" that were little more than patchwork conferences. Charismatic leaders at all levels of the organization came very close to acting in a bureaucratic manner. Nor is the syndicalist structure itself immune to bureaucratic deformations. It was not very difficult for an elaborate network of committees, building up to regional and national bodies, to assume all the features of a centralized organization and circumvent the wishes of the workers' assemblies at the base.

Finally, the CNT, despite its programmatic commitment to libertarian communism and its attempt to function in a libertarian manner, was primarily a large trade union federation rather than a purely anarchist organization. Angel Pestaña, one of its most pragmatic leaders, recognized that roughly a third of the CNT membership could be regarded as anarchists. Many were militants rather than revolutionaries; others simply joined the CNT because it was the dominant union in their area or shop. And by the 1930s, the great majority of CNT members were workers rather than peasants. Andalusians, once the largest percentage of members in the anarchist-influenced unions of the previous century, had dwindled to a minority, a fact which is not noted by such writers as Brenan and Hobsbawm who overemphasize the importance of the rural element in the anarchosyndicalist trade unions.

With the slow change in the social composition of the CNT and the growing supremacy of industrial over village values in its leadership and membership, it is my view that the confederation would have eventually turned into a fairly conventional Latin-type of trade union. The Spanish anarchists were not oblivious to these developments. Although syndicalist unions formed the major arena of anarchist activity in Europe, anarchist theorists were mindful that it would not be too difficult for reformist leaders in syndicalist unions to shift organizational control from the bottom to the top. They viewed syndicalism as a change in focus from the commune to the trade union, from all the oppressed to the industrial proletariat, from the streets to the factories, and, in emphasis at least, from insurrection to the general strike.

Malatesta, fearing the emergence of a bureaucracy in the syndicalist unions, warned that "the official is to the working class a danger only comparable to that provided by the parliamentarian; both lead to corruption and from corruption to death is but a short step." Although he was to change his attitude toward syndicalism, he accepted the movement with many reservations and never ceased to emphasize that "trade unions are, by their very nature, reformist and never revolutionary." To this warning he added that the "revolutionary spirit must be introduced, developed and maintained by the constant actions of revolutionaries who work from within their ranks as well as from outside, but it cannot be the normal, natural definition of the Trade Union's function."

Syndicalism had divided the Spanish anarchist movement without really splitting it. Indeed, until the establishment of the FAI, there was rarely a national anarchist organization to split.[8] Yet a Spanish anarchist movement held together on two levels: by means of well-known periodicals like *La Revista Blanca* and *Tierra y Libertad*, and in the form of small circles of dedicated anarchists, both inside and outside the syndicalist unions. Dating as far back as the 1880s these typically Hispanic groups of intimates, traditionally known as *tertulias*, met at favorite cafes to discuss ideas and plan actions. They gave themselves colorful names expressive of their high-minded ideals *(Ni Rey ni patria)* or their revolutionary spirit *(Los Rebeldes)* or quite simply their sense of fraternity *(Los Afines)*. The Anarchist Organization of the Spanish Region to which I have already alluded, founded in Valencia in 1888, consciously made these *tertulias* the strands from which it tried to weave a coherent movement. Decades later, they were to reappear in the FAI as *grupos de afinidad* (affinity groups) with a more formal local and national structure.

Although Spanish anarchism did not produce an effective national movement until the founding of the FAI, the divisions between the anarchosyndicalists and anarchocommunists were highly significant. The two tendencies of Spanish anarchism worked in very different ways and were mutually disdainful of each other. The anarchosyndicalists functioned directly in the unions. They accepted key union positions and placed their emphasis on organizing, often at the expense of propaganda and ideological commitment. As "practical men," Catalan anarchosyndicalists such as José Rodríguez Romero and Tomás Herreros were ready to make compromises, more precisely, to form alliances with "pure-and-simple" trade unionists.

The anarchocommunists were the "fanatics over there" in the editorial offices of *Tierra y Libertad*—"purists" like Juan Barón and Francisco Cardenal, who regarded the anarchosyndicalists as deserters to reformism and held faithfully to the communist doctrines that formed the basis of the old Anarchist Organization of the Spanish Region. They were not disposed to trade union activism and stressed commitment to libertarian communist principles. It was not their goal to produce a large "mass movement" of workers who wore lightly the trappings of libertarian ideals, but to help create dedicated anarchists in an authentically revolutionary movement, however small its size or influence. Once fairly influential, their terrorist tactics at the turn of the century and the ensuing repression had greatly depleted their numbers.

The founding of the FAI in the summer of 1927 was expected to unite these two tendencies. Anarchosyndicalist needs were met by requiring that every *faísta* become a member of the CNT and by making the union the principal arena of anarchist activity in Spain. The needs of the anarchocommunists were met by the very fact that an avowedly anarchist organization was established nationally, apart from the CNT, and by making the affinity group the basis for a vanguard movement avowedly dedicated to the achievement of libertarian communism.[9] *Tierra y Libertad* was adopted as the FAI's organ. But by establishing an anarchist organization for the express purpose of controlling the CNT, or at least to keep it from falling into the hands of reformists or infiltrators from the newly founded Spanish Communist Party, the anarchosyndicalists had essentially enveloped the anarchocommunists in syndicalist activity. By 1933, the FAI's control over the CNT was fairly complete. Systematic organizational work had purged the union of Communists, while its reformist leaders either left on their own accord or had

To Remember Spain

defensively camouflaged themselves with revolutionary rhetoric. No illusion should exist that this success was achieved with an overly sensitive regard for democratic niceties, although the militancy of the *faístas* unquestionably attracted the greatest majority of CNT workers. But the FAI's most well-known militants —Durruti, the Ascaso brothers, García Oliver—included terrorism in their repertory of direct action. Gunplay, especially in "expropriations" and in dealing with recalcitrant employers, police agents, and blacklegs, was not frowned upon. These *atentados* almost certainly intimidated the FAI's less prominent opponents in the CNT, although "reformists" like Pestaña and Peiró did not hesitate to publicly criticize the FAI in the harshest terms.

Despite its influence in the CNT, this remarkable anarchist organization remained semisecret up to 1936 and its membership probably did not exceed 30,000. Structurally, it formed a near-model of libertarian organization. Affinity groups were small nuclei of intimate friends which generally numbered a dozen or so men and women. Wherever several of these affinity groups existed, they were coordinated by a local federation and met, when possible, in monthly assemblies. The national movement, in turn, was coordinated by a Peninsular Committee, which ostensibly exercised very little directive power. Its role was meant to be strictly administrative in typical Bakuninist fashion. Affinity groups were in fact remarkably autonomous during the early thirties and often exhibited exceptional initiative. The intimacy shared by the *faístas* in each group made the movement very difficult for police agents to infiltrate and the FAI as a whole managed to survive the most severe repression with surprisingly little damage to its organization. As time passed, however, the Peninsular Committee began to grow in prestige. Its periodic statements on events and problems often served as directives to the entire movement. Although by no means an authoritarian body, it eventually began to function as a central committee whose policy decisions, while not binding in the organization, served as more than mere suggestions. Indeed, it would have been very difficult for the Peninsular Committee to operate by fiat; the average *faísta* was a strong personality who would have readily voiced disagreement with any decision that he or she found particularly unpalatable. But the FAI increasingly became an end in itself and loyalty to the organization, particularly when it was under attack or confronted with severe difficulties, tended to mute criticism.

There can be no question that the FAI raised enormously the social consciousness of the average *ceneteista*. More than any single force apart from employer recalcitrance, it made the CNT into a revolutionary syndicalist organization, if not a truly anarchosyndicalist one. The FAI stressed a commitment to revolution and to libertarian communism and gained a considerable following within the CNT (a more dedicated following in anarchist Saragossa than in syndicalist Barcelona). But the FAI was not able to completely rid the CNT of reformist elements (the union attracted many workers by its militant fight for improved economic conditions) and the sedimentation of the CNT along hierarchical lines continued.

In its attempt to control the CNT, the FAI in fact became a victim of the less developed elements in the union. Peirats quite rightly emphasizes that the CNT took its own toll on the FAI. Just as reformists inside the union were predisposed to compromise with the bourgeoisie and the State, so the FAI was compelled to compromise with the reformists in order to retain its control over the CNT. Among the younger, less experienced *faístas*, the situation was sometimes worse. Extravagant militancy which fetishized action over theory and daring over insight rebounded, after failure, in the crudest opportunism.

In the balance: the CNT had provided a remarkably democratic arena for the most militant working class in Europe; the FAI added the leavening of a libertarian orientation and revolutionary deeds within the limits that a trade union could provide. By 1936, both organizations had created authentically libertarian structures to the extent that any strictly proletarian class movement could be truly libertarian. If only by dint of sheer rhetoric — and doubtless, considerable conviction and daring actions — they had keyed the expectations of their memberships to a revolution that would yield workers' control of the economy and syndicalist forms of social administration. This process of education and class organization, more than any single factor in Spain, produced the collectives. And to the degree that the CNT-FAI (for the two

To Remember Spain

organizations became fatally coupled after July 1936) exercised the major influence in an area, the collectives proved to be generally more durable, communist and resistant to Stalinist counterrevolution than other republican-held areas of Spain.

Moreover, in the CNT-FAI areas, workers and peasants tended to show the greatest degree of popular initiative in resisting the military uprising. It was not Socialist Madrid that first took matters into its own hands and defeated its rebellious garrison: it was anarchosyndicalist Barcelona that can lay claim to this distinction among all the large cities of Spain. Madrid rose against the Montana barracks only after sound trucks broadcast the news that the army had been defeated in the streets and squares of Barcelona. And even in Madrid, perhaps the greatest initiative was shown by the local CNT organization, which enjoyed the allegiance of the city's militant construction workers.

The CNT-FAI, in effect, revealed all the possibilities of a highly organized and extremely militant working class — a "classical" proletariat, if you will, whose basic economic interests were repeatedly frustrated by a myopic intransigent bourgeoisie. It was out of such "irreconcilable" struggles that anarcho-syndicalism and revolutionary Marxism had developed their entire tactical and theoretical armamentorium.

But the CNT-FAI also revealed the limitations of that type of classical struggle — and it is fair to say that the Spanish Revolution marked the end of a century-long era of so-called "proletarian revolutions" which began with the June uprising of the Parisian workers in 1848. The era has passed into history and, in my view, will never again be revived. It was marked by bitter, often uncompromising struggles between the proletariat and bourgeoisie, an era in which the working class had not been admitted into its "share" of economic life and had been virtually denied the right to form its own protective institutions. Industrial capitalism in Spain was still a relatively new phenomenon, neither affluent enough to mitigate working class unrest nor sure of its place in political life — yet still asserting an unqualified right to ruthlessly exploit its "hired hands." But this new phenomenon was already beginning to find its way if not toward traditional European liberal political forms, then toward authoritarian ones which would give it the breathing space to develop.

The economic crisis of the thirties (which radicals through-out the world viewed as the final "chronic crisis" of capitalism), coupled with the myopic policies of the Spanish liberals and ruling classes, turned the class struggle in Spain into an explosive class war. The agrarian reform policies of the early thirties republic turned out to be farcical. The liberals were more preoc-cupied with baiting the Church than dealing seriously with the long-range or even short-range economic problems of the penin-sula. The Socialists, who joined the liberals in governing the country, were more concerned with promoting the growth of the UGT at the expense of the CNT than in improving the material conditions of the working class as a whole. The CNT, strongly influenced by volatile *faístas* whose radical education had been acquired in the *pistolero* battles of the early twenties, exploded into repeated insurrections—uprisings which its leaders probably knew were futile, but were meant to stimulate the revolutionary spirit of the working class. These failures by all the elements of Spain in the early republican years to meet the promise of reform left no recourse but revolution and civil war. Except for the most dedicated anarchists, it was a conflict that no one really wanted. But between 1931, when the monarchy was overthrown, and 1936, when the generals rebelled, everyone was sleep-walking into the last of the great proletarian revolutions — perhaps the greatest in terms of its short-lived social programs and the initiative shown by the oppressed. The era seemed to have collected all its energies, its traditions, and its dreams for its last great confrontation — and thereafter was to disappear.

It is not surprising that the most communistic collectives in the Spanish Revolution appeared in the countryside rather than the cities, among villagers who were still influenced by archaic collectivistic traditions and were less ensnared in a market economy than their urban cousins. The ascetic values which so greatly influenced these highly communistic collectives often reflected the extreme poverty of the areas in which they were rooted. Cooperation and mutual aid in such cases formed the preconditions for survival of the community. Elsewhere, in the more arid areas of Spain, the need for sharing water and main-taining irrigation works was an added inducement to collective

farming. Here, collectivization was also a technological necessity, but one which even the republic did not interfere with. What
makes these rural collectives important is not only that many of
them practiced communism, but that they functioned so
effectively under a system of popular self-management. This
belies the notion held by so many authoritarian Marxists that
economic life must be scrupulously "planned" by a highly
centralized state power and the odious canard that popular collectivization, as distinguished from statist nationalization,
necessarily pits collectivized enterprises against each other in
competition for profits and resources.

In the cities, however, collectivization of the factories, com-
munications systems, and transport facilities took a very different form. Initially nearly the entire economy in CNT-FAI areas
had been taken over by committees elected from among the
workers and were loosely coordinated by higher union committees. As time went on this system was increasingly tightened.
The higher committee began to preempt the initiative to the
lower although their decisions still had to be ratified by the
workers of the facilities involved. The effect of this process was
to tend to centralize the economy of CNT-FAI areas in the hands
of the union. The extent to which this process unfolded varied
greatly from industry to industry and area to area, and with the
limited knowledge we have at hand, generalizations are very
difficult to formulate. With the entry of the CNT-FAI into the
Catalan government in 1936, the process of centralization continued and the union-controlled facilities became wedded to the
state. By early 1938 a political bureaucracy had largely sup-
planted the authority of the workers' committees in all "republican"-held cities. Although workers' control existed in theory, it
had virtually disappeared in fact.

If the commune formed the basis for the rural collectives, the
committee formed the basis for the industrial collectives. Indeed,
apart from the rural communes, the committee system predominated wherever the State power had collapsed — in villages and
towns as well as factories and urban neighborhoods. "All had
been set up in the heat of action to direct the popular response to
the military coup d'état," observe Pierre Broué and Emile Témime:

To Remember Spain

They had been appointed in an infinite number of ways. In the villages, the factories, and on the work sites, time had sometimes been taken to elect them, at least summarily, at a general meeting. At all events, care had been taken to see that all parties and unions were represented on them, even if they did not exist before the Revolution, because the Committee represented at one and the same time as the workers a whole and the sum total of their organizations: in more than one place those elected came to an understanding as to who was to represent one or another union, who would be the "Republican" and who the "Socialist." Very often, in the towns, the most active elements appointed themselves. It was sometimes the electors as a whole who chose the men to sit on the Committee of each organization, but more often the members of the Committee were elected either by a vote within their own organization or were quite simply appointed by the local governing committees of the parties and unions.

The nearly forty years that separate our own time from the Spanish revolution have produced sweeping changes in Western Europe and America, changes that are also reflected in Spain's present social development. The classical proletariat that fought so desperately for the minimal means of life is giving way to a more affluent worker whose main concern is not material survival and employment, but a more human way of life and meaningful work. The social composition of the labor force is changing as well — proportionately, more toward commercial, service, and professional vocations than unskilled labor in mass manufacturing industries. Spain, like the rest of Western Europe, is no longer predominantly an agricultural country; the majority of its people live in towns and cities, not in the relatively isolated villages that nourished rural collectivism. In a visit to working class Barcelona during the late sixties, I seemed to see as many American-style attaché cases as lunch boxes.

These changes in the goals and traits of the nonbourgeois classes in capitalist society are the products of the sweeping industrial revolution that followed the Second World War and of the relative affluence or expectations of affluence that have brought all the values of material scarcity into question They have introduced a historic tension between the irrationality of present lifeways and the utopian promise of a liberated society. The young workers of the late sixties and early seventies tend to borrow their values from relatively affluent middle-class youth, who no longer hypostasize the work ethic, puritanical mores, hierarchical obedience, and material security, but rather free time for self-development, sexual liberation in the broadest sense of the term, creative or stimulating work as distinguished from mindless labor, and an almost libidinal disdain for all authority. In Spain it is significant that privileged university students, who tended to play a reactionary role in the thirties, are among the most radical elements of society in the sixties and seventies. Together with young workers and intellectuals in all fields, they are beginning to accept in varying degrees the personalistic and utopistic goals that make the puritanical and overly institutionalized anarchosyndicalism of the CNT-FAI seem anachronistic.

The limitations of the trade union movement, even in its anarchosyndicalist form, have become manifestly clear. To see in trade unions (whether syndicalist or not) an inherent potentiality for revolutionary struggle is to assume that the interests of workers and capitalists, *merely as classes*, are intrinsically incompatible. This is demonstrably untrue if one is willing to acknowledge the obvious capacity of the system to remake or to literally create the worker in the image of a repressive industrial culture and rationality. From the family, through the school and religious institutions, the mass media, to the factory and finally trade union and "revolutionary" party, capitalist society conspires to foster obedience, hierarchy, the work ethic, and authoritarian discipline in the working class as a whole; indeed, in many of its "emancipatory" movements as well.

The factory and the class organizations that spring from it play the most the compelling role in promoting a well-regulated, almost unconscious docility in mature workers — a docility that manifests itself not so much in characterless passivity as in a pragmatic commitment to hierarchical organizations and authoritarian leaders. Workers can be very militant and exhibit strong, even powerful character traits in the most demanding social situations; but these traits can be brought as much, if not more readily, to the service of a reformist labor bureaucracy as to a libertarian revolutionary movement. They must break with the hold of bourgeois culture on their sensibilities — specifically, with the hold of the factory, the locus of the workers' very *class* existence — before they can move into that supreme form of direct action called "revolution," and further, construct a society they will *directly* control in their workshops and communities.

This amounts to saying that workers must see themselves as human beings, not as class beings; as creative personalities, not as "proletarians"; as self-affirming individuals, not as "masses." And the destiny of a liberated society must be the free commune, not the confederation of factories, however self-administered; for such a confederation takes a part of society — its economic component — and reifies it into the totality of society. Indeed, even that economic component must be humanized precisely by our bringing an "affinity of friendship" to the work process, by diminishing the role of onerous work in the lives of the producers, indeed, by a total "transvaluation of values" (to use Nietzsche's phrase) as it applies to production and consumption as well as social and personal life.

Even though certain aspects of the libertarian revolution in Spain have lost their relevance, anarchist concepts themselves that can encompass and fully express a "post-scarcity mentality" can be much more relevant to the present than the authoritarian ideologies of the 1930s, despite the tendency of these ideologies to fill the vacuum left by the absence of meaningful libertarian alternatives and organizations. Such anarchist concepts could no longer rely in practical terms on the collectivist traditions of the countryside; these traditions are virtually gone as living forces although perhaps the memory of the old collectivist traditions lives among Spanish youth in the same sense that American youth have turned to the tribal traditions of the American Indians for cultural inspiration. With the decline of the nuclear family and in reaction to urban atomization, the commune has everywhere acquired a new relevance for young and even older people — a shared, mutually supportive way of life based on *selective* affinity rather than kinship ties. Burgeoning urbanization has posed more sharply than ever the need for decentralistic alternatives to the megalopolis; the gigantism of the city, the need for the human scale. The grotesque bureaucratization of life, which in Camus's words reduces everyone to a functionary, has placed a new value on nonauthoritarian institutions and direct action. Slowly, even amidst the setbacks of our time, a new self is being forged. Potentially, this is a libertarian self that could intervene directly in the changing and administration of society — a self that could engage in the self-discipline, self-activity, and self-management so crucial to the development of a truly free society. Here the values prized so highly by traditional anarchocommunism establish direct continuity with a contemporary form of anarchocommunism that gives consciousness and coherence to the intuitive impulses of this new sensibility.

But if these goals are to be achieved, contemporary anarchocommunism cannot remain a mere mood or tendency, wafting in the air like a cultural ambiance It must be organized — indeed, *well*-organized — if it is to effectively articulate and spread this new sensibility; it must have a coherent theory and extensive literature; it must be capable of dueling with the authoritarian movements that try to denature the intuitive libertarian impulses of our time and channel social unrest into hierarchical forms of organization. On this score, Spanish anarchism is profoundly relevant for our time, and the Spanish Revolution still provides the most valuable lessons in the problem of self-management that we can cull from the past.

To deal with these problems, perhaps I can best begin by saying that there is little, in fact, to criticize in the structural forms that the CNT and the FAI tried to establish. The CNT, almost from the outset, organized its locals as factory rather than craft unions, and the nationwide occupational federations (the *Uniones de oficio*, or "internationals" as we would call them) which emerged with the IWMA were abandoned for local federations (the *Federaciones locales*). This structure situated the factory in the community, where it really belonged if the "commune" concept was to be realistic, rather than in an easily manipulatable industrial network that easily lent itself to statist nationalization The *centros obreros*, the local federations, the careful mandating of delegates to congresses, the elimination of paid officials, the establishment of regional federations, regional committees, and even a National

Committee, would all have been in conformity with libertarian principles had all of these institutions lived up their intentions. Where the CNT structure failed most seriously was in the need to convene frequent assemblies of workers at the local level, and similarly, frequent national and regional conferences to continually reevaluate CNT policies and prevent power from collecting in the higher committees. For as frequent as meetings may have been — committees, subcommittees, and regional and national committee meetings — the regular and close communication between workers and the "influential militants" did tend to become ruptured.

Confusion developed over the crucial problem of the locus for making policy decisions. The real place for this process should have been shop assemblies, regular congresses, or when events and circumstances required rapid decisions, conferences of clearly mandated and recallable delegates elected for this purpose by the membership. The sole responsibility of the regional and national committees should have been administrative — that is, the coordination and execution of policy decisions formulated by membership meetings and conference or congress delegates.

Nevertheless, the structure of the CNT as a syndicalist union and that of the FAI as an anarchist federation was, in many respects, quite admirable. Indeed, my principal criticisms in the pages above have been not so much of the forms themselves, but of the departures the CNT and the FAI made from them. Perhaps even more significantly, I've tried to explain the social limitations of the period — including the mystique about the classical proletariat — that vitiated the realization of these structural forms.

Another issue that was a crucial problem for the FAI and which is still a source of confusion for anarchists at the present time is the problem of the "influential militant" — the more informed, experienced, "strong," and oratorically gifted individuals who tended to formulate policy at all levels of the organization.

It will never be possible to eliminate the fact that human beings have different levels of knowledge and consciousness. Our prolonged period of dependence as children, the fact that we are largely the products of an acquired culture and that experience tends to confer knowledge on the older person would lead to such differences even in the most liberated society. In hierarchical societies, the dependence of the less-informed on the more-informed is commonly a means of manipulation and power. The older, more experienced person, like the parent, has this privilege at his or her disposal and, with it, an alternative: to use knowledge, experience, and oratorical gifts as means of domination and to induce adulation — or for the goal of lovingly imparting knowledge and experience, for equalizing the relationship between teacher and taught, and always leaving the less experienced and informed individual free to make his or her decisions.

Hegel brilliantly draws the distinction between Socrates and Jesus: the former was a teacher who sought to arouse a quest for knowledge in anyone who was prepared to discuss; the latter, an oracle who pronounced for adoring disciples to interpret exegetically. The difference, as Hegel points out, lay not only in the character of the two men but in that of their "followers." Socrates' friends had been reared in a social tradition that "developed their powers in many directions. They had absorbed that democratic spirit which gives an individual a greater measure of independence and makes it impossible for any tolerably good head to depend wholly and absolutely on one person. . . . They loved Socrates because of his virtue and his philosophy, not virtue and his philosophy because of him." The followers of Jesus, on the other hand, were submissive acolytes: "Lacking any great store of spiritual energy of their own, they had found the basis of their conviction about the teaching of Jesus principally in their friendship with him and dependence on him. They had not attained truth and freedom by their own exertions; only by laborious learning had they acquired a dim sense of them and certain formulas about them. Their ambition was to grasp and keep this doctrine faithfully and to transmit it equally faithfully to others without any addition, without letting it acquire any variations in detail by working on it themselves."

The FAI — illegal by choice, sometimes terrorist in its tactics, and aggressively "macho" in its almost competitive daring — developed deeply personal ties within its affinity groups. Durruti's grief for the death of Francisco Ascaso revealed real love, not merely the friendship that stems from organizational collaboration. But in the FAI both friendship and love were often based on a demanding association, one that implicitly required conformity to the most "heroic" standards established by the most "daring" militants in the group. Such relationships are not likely to shatter over doctrinal disagreements or what often seem like "mere" points of theory. Eventually these relationships produce leaders and led; worse, the leaders tended to patronize the led and finally manipulate them.

To escape this process of devolution, an anarchist organization must be aware of the fact that the process *can* occur, and it must be vigilant against its occurrence. To be effective, the vigilance must eventually express itself in more positive terms. It cannot coexist with an adulation of violence, competitive daring, and mindless aggressiveness, not to speak of an equally mindless worship of activism and "strong characters." The organization must recognize that differences in experiences and consciousness *do* exist among its members and handle these differences with a wary consciousness — not conceal them with euphemisms like "influential militant." The taught as well as the teacher must first ask himself or herself whether domination and manipulation is being practiced — and not to deny that a systematic teaching process is taking place. Moreover, everyone must be fully aware that this teaching process is unavoidable within the movement if relationships are eventually to be equalized by imparted knowledge and the fruits of experience. To a large extent, the conclusions one arrives about the nature of this process are almost intuitively determinable by the behavior patterns that develop between comrades. Ultimately, under conditions of freedom, social intercourse, friendship, and love would be of the "free-giving" kind that Jacob Bachofen imputed to "matriarchal" society, not the demanding censorious type he associated with patriarchy. Here, the affinity group or commune would achieve the most advanced and libertarian expression of its humanity. Merely to strive for this goal among its own brothers and sisters would qualitatively distinguish it from other movements and provide the most assurable guarantee that it would remain true to its libertarian principles.

Our period, which stresses the development of the individual self as well as social self-management, stands in a highly advantageous position to assess the authentic nature of libertar-

To Remember Spain

ian organization and relationships. A European or American civil war of the kind that wasted Spain in the thirties is no longer conceivable in an epoch that can deploy nuclear weapons, supersonic aircraft, nerve gas, and a terrifying firepower against revolutionaries. Capitalist institutions must be hollowed out by a molecular historical process of disengagement and disloyalty to a point where any popular majoritarian movement can cause them to collapse for want of support and moral authority. But the kind of development such a change will produce — whether it will occur consciously or not, whether it will have an authoritarian outcome or one based on self-management — will depend very much upon whether a conscious, well-organized libertarian movement can emerge.

Notes

1. Both the UGT and the CNT probably numbered more than a million members each by the summer of 1936. The officious, highly bureaucratic UGT tended to overstate its membership figures. The more amorphous decentralized CNT—the more persecuted of the two labor federations — often exercised much greater influence on the Spanish working class than its membership statistics would seem to indicate.
2. Madrid, although with a largely Socialist labor movement, was the home of an intensely active anarchist movement. Not only were the Madrid construction workers strongly anarchosyndicalist, but at the turn of the century, many Madrid intellectuals were committed to anarchism and established a renowned theoretical tradition for the movement that lingered on long after anarchist workers had cut their ties with the Spanish intelligentsia.
3. I would not want to argue here, that the Spanish village formed a *paradigm* for a libertarian society. Village society differed greatly from one region of Spain to another — some areas retaining undisturbed their local democratic traditions, others ruled tyrannically by the Church, the nobility, *caciques*, and custom. Quite often, both tendencies coexisted in a very uneasy equilibrium, the democratic still vital but submerged by the authoritarian.
4. In the case of the CNT there were exceptions to this rule. The National Secretary was paid an average worker's salary, as was the clerical staff of the National Committee and the editors and staffs of

daily newspapers. But delegates to the national, regional, and local committees of the CNT were not paid and were obliged to work at their own trades except when they lost time during working hours on union business. This is not to say that there were no individuals who devoted most of their time to the dissemination of anarchist ideas. "Traveling about from place to place, on foot or mule or on the hard seats of third-class railway carriages, or even like tramps or ambulant bullfighters under the tarpaulins of goods wagons," observes Brenan, "whilst they organized new groups or carried on propagandist campaigns, these 'apostles of the idea,' as they were called, lived like mendicant friars on the hospitality of the more prosperous workers" — and, I would add, "villagers." This tradition of organizing, which refers to the 1870s, did not disappear in later decades; to the contrary, it became more systematic and perhaps more securely financed as the CNT began to compete with the UGT for the allegiance of the Spanish workers and peasants.

5. Yet here I must add that to abstain from smoking, to live by high moral standards, and especially to abjure the consumption of alcohol was very important at the time. Spain was going through her own belated industrial revolution during the period of anarchist ascendancy with all its demoralizing features. The collapse of morale among the proletariat, with rampant drunkenness and venereal diseases, and the collapse of sanitary facilities, was the foremost problem which Spanish revolutionaries had to deal with, just as black radicals today must deal with similar problems in the ghetto. On this score, the Spanish anarchists were eminently successful. Few CNT workers, much less committed anarchists, would have dared to show up drunk at meetings or misbehave overtly among their comrades. If one considers the terrible working and living conditions of the period, alcoholism was not as serious a problem in Spain as it was in England during the industrial revolution.

6. In "black" (purely anarchistic) Saragossa, where the working class was even more firmly committed to anarchist principles than the Barcelona proletariat, Raymond Carr quite accurately emphasizes that "strikes were characterized by their scorn for economic demands and the toughness of their revolutionary solidarity: strikes for comrades in prison were more popular than strikes for better conditions."

7. For Marx and Engels, organizational forms to change the behavioral patterns of the proletariat were not a problem. This question could be

postponed until "after the revolution." Indeed, Marx viewed the authoritarian impact of the factory ("the very mechanism of the process of capitalist production itself") as a positive factor in producing a disciplined, united proletariat. Engels, in an atrocious diatribe against the anarchists titled "On Authority," explicitly used the factory structure — its hierarchical forms and the obedience it demanded — to justify his commitment to authority and centralization in working-class organizations. What is of interest here is not whether Marx and Engels were "authoritarians" but the way in which they thought out the problem of proletarian organization — the extent to which the matrix for their organizational concepts was the very economy which the social revolution was meant to revolutionize.

8. The disappearance of Bakunin's Alliance of Social Democracy in Spain scattered the forces of Spanish anarchism into small local nuclei which related on a regional basis through conferences, periodicals, and correspondence. Several regional federations of these nuclei were formed, mainly in Catalonia and Andalusia, only to disappear as rapidly as they emerged.

9. I employ the word "vanguard" provocatively, despite its unpopularity in many libertarian circles today, because this term was widely used in the traditional anarchist movement. Some anarchist publications even adopted it as a name. There can be no doubt that an anarchist *obrera consciente* regarded himself or herself as an "advanced person" and part of a small *avant-garde* in society. In its most innocuous sense, the use of this term meant that such a person merely enjoyed a more advanced social consciousness than the majority of less developed workers and peasants, a distinction that had to be overcome by education. In a less innocuous sense, the word provided a rationale for elitism and manipulation, to which some anarchist leaders were no more immune than their authoritarian Socialist opponents. The word "leader," on the other hand, was eschewed for the euphemism "influential militant," although in fact the more well-known anarchist "influential militants" were certainly leaders. This self-deception was not as trifling as it may seem. It prevented the Spanish anarchists from working out the serious problems that emerged from real differences in consciousness among themselves or between themselves and the great majority of undeveloped *ceneteistas*.

To Remember Spain

After Fifty Years:
The Spanish Civil War

Between myth and reality there lies a precarious zone of transition that occasionally captures the truth of each. Spain, caught in a world-historic revolution fifty years ago, was exactly such an occasion — a rare moment when the most generous, almost mythic dreams of freedom seemed suddenly to become real for millions of Spanish workers, peasants, and intellectuals. For this brief period of time, this shimmering moment, as it were, the world stood breathlessly still, while the red banners of revolutionary socialism and the red-and-black banners of revolutionary anarchosyndicalism floated over most of Spain's major cities and thousands of her villages.

Taken together with the massive, spontaneous collectivization of factories, fields, even hotels and restaurants, the oppressed classes of Spain reclaimed history with a force and passion of an unprecedented scope and gave a stunning reality in many areas of the peninsula to the ageless dream of a free society. The Spanish Civil War of 1936-39 was, at its inception, the last of the classical European workers' and peasants' revolutions — not, let me make it clear, a short-lived "uprising," a cadre-controlled "guerrilla war," or a simple civil conflict between regions for national supremacy. And like so many life-forms that appear for the last time, before fading away forever, it was the most far-reaching and challenging of all such popular movements of the great revolutionary era that encompasses Cromwellian England of the late 1640s and the working-class uprisings of Vienna and Asturias of the early 1930s.

It is not a myth but a sheer lie — the cretinous perversion of history by its makers in the academy — to depict the Spanish Civil War as a mere prelude to World War II, an alleged conflict between "democracy and fascism." Not even World War II deserves the honor of this ideological characterization. Spain was seized by more than a civil war: it was in the throes of a profound social revolution. Nor was this revolution, like so many self-styled ones of recent years, simply the product of Spain's struggle for modernization. If anything, Spain was one of those very rare countries where problems of modernization helped inspire a *real* social revolution rather than a reaction or adaptation to Western and Eastern Europe's economic and social development. This seemingly "Third World" feature of the Spanish Civil War and, above all, the extraordinary alternatives it posed to capitalism and authoritarian forms of socialism make the revolution hauntingly relevant to liberation movements today. In modernizing the country, the Spanish working class and peasantry literally took over much of its economy and managed it directly in the form of collectives, cooperatives, and union-networked syndicalist structures. Democratically-run militias, free of all ranking distinctions and organized around a joint decision-making process that involved the soldiers as well as their elected "commanders," moved rapidly to the military fronts.

To have stopped Franco's "Army of Africa," composed of foreign legionnaires and Moorish mercenaries — perhaps the blood-thirstiest and certainly one of the most professionalized troops at the disposal of any European nation at the time — and its well-trained Civil Guards and police auxiliaries, would have been nothing less than miraculous once it established a strong base on the Spanish mainland. That hastily formed, untrained, and virtually unequipped militiamen and women slowed up Franco's army's advance on Madrid for four months and essentially stopped it on the outskirts of the capital is a feat for which they have rarely earned the proper tribute from writers on the civil war of the past half century.

Behind the "Republican" lines, power lay essentially in the hands of the trade unions and their political organizations: the million-member General Confederation of Workers (UGT), the labor federation of the Socialist Workers Party (PSOE), and the equally large General Confederation of Labor (CNT), strongly influenced by the semi-clandestine Iberian Anarchist Federation (FAI). Additionally, another leftist organization, the Workers Party of Marxist Unification (POUM), whose more radical members and leaders had been rooted in a Trotskyist tradition in earlier years, followed up the more influential socialists and anarchists. In Catalonia, the POUM outnumbered by far the Communist and Socialist Parties which united to form the predominantly Communist-controlled Unified Socialist Party of Catalonia (PSUC). The Communist Party (PCE) at the inception of the revolution was inconsequential in numbers and influence, lagging far behind the three major left-wing organizations and their unions.

The wave of collectivizations that swept over Spain in the summer and autumn of 1936 has been described in a recent BBC-Granada documentary as "the greatest experiment in workers' self-management Western Europe has ever seen," a revolution more far-reaching than any which occurred in Russia during 1917-21 and the years before and after it.[1] In anarchist industrial areas like Catalonia, an estimated three-quarters of the economy was placed under workers' control, as it was in anarchist rural areas like Aragon. The figure tapers downward where the UGT shared power with the CNT or else predominated: 50 percent in anarchist and socialist Valencia, and 30 percent in socialist and liberal Madrid. In the more thoroughly anarchist areas, particularly among the agrarian collectives, money was eliminated and the material means of life were allocated strictly according to need rather than work, following the traditional precepts of a libertarian communist society. As the BBC-Granada television documentary puts it: "The ancient dream of a collective society without profit or property was made reality in the villages of Aragon.... All forms of production were owned by the community, run by their workers."

The administrative apparatus of "Republican" Spain belonged almost entirely to the unions and their political organizations. Police in many cities were replaced by armed workers' patrols. Militia units were formed everywhere—in factories, on farms, and in socialist and anarchist community centers and union halls, initially including women as well as men. A vast network of local revolutionary committees coordinated the feeding of the cities, the operations of the economy, and the meting out of justice, indeed, almost every facet of Spanish life from production to culture, bringing the whole of Spanish society in the "Republican" zone into a well-organized and coherent whole. This historically unprecedented appropriation of society by its most oppressed sectors — including women, who were liberated from all the constraints of a highly traditional Catholic country, be it the prohibition of abortion and divorce or a degraded status in the economy — was the work of the Spanish proletariat and peasantry. It was a movement from below that overwhelmed even the revolutionary organizations of the oppressed, including the CNT-FAI. "Significantly, no left organization issued calls for revolutionary takeovers of factories, workplaces or the land," observes Ronald Fraser in one of the most up-to-date accounts of the popular movement. "Indeed, the CNT leadership in Barcelona, epicenter of urban anarchosyndicalism, went further: rejecting the offer of power presented to it by President Companys [the head of the Catalan government], it decided that the libertarian revolution must stand aside for collaboration with the Popular Front forces to defeat the common enemy. The revolution that transformed Barcelona in a matter of days into a city virtually run by the working class sprang initially from individual CNT unions, impelled by their most advanced militants; and as their example spread it was not only large enterprises but small workshops and businesses that were being taken over.[2]

I quote Fraser to emphasize the remarkable power of education and discussion, and the critical examination of experience in the development of many segments of the Spanish working class and peasantry. For Communists like Eric Hobsbawn to designate these segments, largely influenced by anarchist ideas, as "primitive rebels" is worse than prejudice; it represents ideology mechanically imposed on the flux of history, organizing it into "stages" of development in flat contradiction to real life and freezing it into categories that exist solely in the mind of the historian. Since Spain, as we are told, was a predominately agrarian country, in fact, "feudal" in its social structure, its proletariat must have been "undeveloped" and its peasantry caught in a fever of "millennarian" expectations. These "primitive" features of Spain's development somehow account, so the story goes, for the more than one million members of the anarchosyndicalist CNT out of a population of twenty-four million. Spain's bourgeoisie, it is further argued, was the cowed stepchild of the country's territorial grandees, its clerics, and its bloated officer corps; Spain needed a "bourgeois-democratic" revolution, akin to the French and American, as a "historical precondition" for a "socialist" one. This "stages theory," with its salad of "preconditions," was invoked with considerable effectiveness by the Communist International in the 1930s against the reality of an authentic workers' and peasants' revolution. Where it could not be completely concealed from the outside world, the revolution was denounced by the Communists as "premature" in a "balance of history" that was determined somewhere in the foreign commissariat of Stalinist Russia and resolutely assaulted by the PCE on a scale that brought "Republican" Spain to the edge of a civil war within the civil war.

Recent accounts of Spain and the revolution of 1936 give us a very different picture of the country's society from its portrayal by the Communists, their liberal allies, and even by such well-intentioned observers as Gerald Brenan and Franz Borkenau. Despite its outward trappings, Spain was not the overwhelmingly agrarian and "feudal" country we were taught it was two generations ago. From the turn of the century to the coming of the Second Republic in 1931, Spain had undergone enormous economic growth with major changes in the relative weight of the agricultural and nonagricultural sectors. From 1910 to 1930 the peasantry had declined from 66 percent to 45.5 percent of the working population, while industrial workers had soared from 15.8 percent to 26.5 percent and those in services from 18.1 percent to 27.9 percent. Indeed, the peasantry now formed a minority of the population, not its traditional majority, and a substantial portion of the "peasantry" owned land, particularly in areas that adhered to the highly conservative "National Front" as against the liberal-socialist-communist coalition under the rubric of the "Popular Front." Indeed, omitting the Center parties the "Popular Front" — whose election in February 1936 precipitated the military plots that led to the Francoist rebellion six months later — received only 54 percent of the vote in a voting procedure and under circumstances that favored them. Moreover, as Edward Malefakis has shown in his thoroughly researched study of agrarian unrest in the period leading up to the civil war, the CNT had its greatest strength among the industrial working class of Catalonia, not among the "millennarian" agricultural day-workers of the South. Many of these *braceros* joined socialist unions in the 1930s, pushing the reformist Socialist party in an increasingly revolutionary direction.[3]

Spain's rapid rate of industrialization and the shift of the country from "feudal" to essentially capitalist forms of agriculture occurred well in advance of the "Popular Front" victory. The decade of the 1920s under the fairly indulgent, Mussolini-type dictatorship of Primo de Rivera (a Spanish parody of Italian fascism in which leading Socialists like Largo Caballero actually held official positions as did other UGT chieftains), saw an economic modernization of the country that almost equaled and in some cases exceeded the boom years under Franco between 1960 and 1973. Illiteracy was substantially decreased, and economic expansion was accelerated; hence the very sizable middle class or service workers with middle-class values that could be played against the militant working class of Spain.

The greatest single reservoir of economic unrest was in the south: Andalusia's plantation or *latifundia* society, structured around the cultivation of olives, cereals, grapes — and the large workforce of desperately poor, half-starved landless day-laborers. Caught in the trammels of Spain's quasifeudal grandees, hundreds of thousands of *braceros* lived in bitter desperation, a way of life that contrasted with the opulence and cold arrogance of the royalist upper class of nobles and bourgeois who were to form the cutting edge of Franco's rebellion and were the principal beneficiaries of his victory.

Periodic uprisings of the *braceros* had culminated in an agrarian war in 1918-20 and were put down mercilessly, leaving a legacy of savage class hatred that expressed itself in the burning of crops, farm buildings, and rural mansions (many of which were turned into virtual fortresses during times of social unrest), and assassinations on both sides of the class barrier. Long before the 1930s, Andalusia became, for all practical purposes, an occupied territory where Civil Guards patrolled the countryside and, together with armed thugs hired by landowners, fired wantonly at striking *braceros* and created the endemic violence that claimed an appalling toll during the first weeks of the civil war. Yet here too, agriculture was largely capitalistic in its orientation toward the marketplace. Andalusia's produce was cultivated largely for international trade. Noble titles often concealed bourgeois avarice in its most unfeeling form, and upper-class references to the "tradition" of Spain barely camouflaged pernicious greed and privilege.

What cannot be ignored after presenting this tableau is the extent to which the crisis that led to the 1936 revolution was cultural as well as economic. Spain was a land of several nations: Basques and Catalans who sought autonomy for their respective cultures and viewed Spanish lifeways with a measure of disdain; Castilians who appeared as the collective oppressors of the peninsula, despite their own internal divisions; an arrogant nobility that fed on images of Spain's "golden era" and lived in almost parochial isolation from the real Spain that surrounded them; an incestuous officer caste that belonged to one of the country's lingering "orders" and for whom "national regeneration" had devolved from the values of liberalism and "modernity" to those of sheer reaction; finally, a virtually medieval Church that was excessively propertied, rigidly hierarchical, and often bitterly hated because of the contrast between its pious rhetoric of human "brotherhood" and its patent partisanship with the upper classes.

Above all, Spain was a land in which cultures were in dramatic transition between town and country, feudalism and capitalism — a nostalgic world that looked back to a past of aristocratic supremacy and forward to a future of plebeian egalitarianism that found its most radical form in a huge anarchosyndicalist movement. What made the Spanish working class so uniquely revolutionary, in my view, was its well-rooted ancestry in the countryside — in a relatively slow-paced, organic agrarian world that clashed sharply with the highly rationalized, mechanized industrial world of the cities. In the force-field of these two cultures, Spanish workers in the Mediterranean coastal cities retained an obduracy, a sense of moral tension, a feeling for preindustrial lifeways, and a commitment to community that cannot be conveyed to a generation immured in the received wisdom and prepackaged lifeways of a highly commodified, market-oriented era.

The intensity of this force-field was heightened by a Spanish heritage of strong sociability: urban *barrios* were actually intimate villages within the city, knitted together by cafes, community centers and union halls and energized by a vital outdoor public life that stood at sharp variance with the aristocratic mythos of the Spanish past and the hated Church which had abdicated all claims to public service. The elite classes of the country, so completely divorced from those who worked for them, were highly protective of the privileges conferred upon them by pedigree, status, and landed wealth, which often produced fissures as bourgeois parvenus began to enter a social terrain guarded for centuries by tradition and history.

Accordingly, one *always* "belonged" in a deeply social, cultural, regional, class, and economic sense — whether it was to a part of Spain, to a hierarchy, a caste, a clan, an institution (be it the army or a union), and finally, to a neighborhood, village, town, city, and province, precisely in that order of loyalty. In this cultural sense affiliations and antagonisms often overrode economic considerations to an extent that is now barely comprehensible To cite only one example, the workers of Saragossa, even more anarchist in their ideology than their syndicalistic comrades in Barcelona, disdained strikes for "paltry" economic demands; they normally put down their tools in behalf of their brothers and sisters in prisons or over issues of politics, human rights, and class solidarity. In one truly incredible instance, these "pure" anarchists declared a twenty-four-hour general-strike because the German Communist leader, Ernst Thälmann, had been arrested by Hitler.

Behind this vibrantly radical culture was a rich tradition of direct action, self-management, and confederal association. Spain had barely become a nation-state under Ferdinand and Isabella

— the "Catholic monarchs" who conquered the last Moorish strongholds on the peninsula — when the monarchy was faced with a historic crisis. Under the *Comuneros* (translated literally, the Communards), Castile's major cities rose up in revolt to demand what was virtually a form of nationhood structured primarily around a confederation of municipalities. In this remarkable moment when a confederal political system hovered as an alternative to a centralized nation-state, Castilian cities created short-lived ward democracies and neighborhood assemblies and enfranchised people in the lowest ranks of the community on a scale that would have sent a shudder of fear through Europe's ruling elites, possibly comparable to the impact of the Paris Commune of 1871.[4] Such confederal movements percolated through Spanish history for generations . They took real-life form in the extraordinary power of local society over centralized state institutions, exploding in movements like the Federalists of Pi y Margall of the early 1870s and the anarchists schooled in the writings of Bakunin. But Spanish localism and confederalism were not strictly an anarchist phenomenon: they were Spanish to the core and infused the most traditional socialists, even the Basque nationalists, who advanced municipalist notions of political control against the centralized state's authority well into the 1930s.

Spanish radicalism, in effect, raised questions and provided answers that have a unique relevance to the problems of our day: local autonomy, confederalism, collectivism, self-management, and base democracy in opposition to state centralism, nationalization, managerial control, and bureaucracy. The world did not know this in 1936, nor does it understood the scope of these issues adequately today. Indeed, Spanish radicalism also raised ideological images that history rendered obsolete in Europe: images of a classical proletarian insurrection, barricades, a syndicalist triumph of revolutionary trade unions, and inchoate notions of emancipation cloaked in a Bolshevik mantle claimed by Stalin rather than in Spain's own popular traditions. It was this swirling vortex of social dislocations that the Spanish army tried to still, a vortex of institutional relics, an agrarian crisis where large-scale agribusiness dressed in aristocratic vestments was pitted against a ragged, land-hungry, labor force of day-workers, and an arrogant nobility, an avaricious bourgeoisie, an inordinately materialistic Church, and a servile middle class against the most volatile proletariat and peasantry Europe had seen in a century of revolutionary anarchism and socialism.

The events leading to the outbreak of civil war can be dealt with summarily. In Spain, history seems to repeat itself first as farce and only later as tragedy. The social dislocations that followed World War I seem almost a comic anticipation of the developments that preceded Franco's uprising. A wave of revolutionary unrest gave way in 1923 to the military dictatorship of General Primo de Rivera, a pleasure-loving, rather dissolute Andalusian aristocrat who easily came to terms with the UGT and the Socialists at the expense of their anarchosyndicalist rivals and who essentially ignored the Spanish Communist Party because of its sheer insignificance. The boom years of the 1920s were followed by a rapid decline in Primo's authoritarian government, which pulled the props out from underneath the monarchy itself. In April 1931 Spain returned after some two generations to a republican political system, seemingly with almost universal enthusiasm — but the system's authority waned quickly when a liberal-Socialist coalition tried to address the crucial agrarian problems that had beleaguered all Spanish governments for generations. Hammered on the right by the attempted military coup of General Sanjurjo (August 1932) and by anarchosyndicalist insurrectionism on the left which culminated in the Casas Viejas massacre of Andalusian peasants (January 1933), the coalition lay in the debris of its own ill-starred reforms.

In the summer of 1933, Spain's multitude of parties and organizations began to regroup and polarize. In November of that year, a coalition of the right, the Spanish Confederation of Right Groups (CEDA) replaced the liberal-Socialist coalition headed by Manuel Azaña. The forces that consigned the first "Republican" government in some sixty years to the historic garbage heap now formed the impetus for a radical shift to the two extremes. Disenchanted with liberal ineptitude and subjected to increasing internal pressure by the influx of Andalusian *braceros*, the Socialist Party veered sharply from reformism to revolutionism in little more than a year. Just as the CEDA found the newly formed fascistic Falange on its far right, so Largo Cabellero (now styled the "Lenin of Spain") found the recent POUM, a melding of two independent revolutionary Marxist groups, on his far left and the anarchosyndicalists in a state of chronic revolution still further off on their own.

The barricades that the Viennese Socialist workers raised early in 1934 in the face of a reactionary assault on their very existence had their bloody Spanish counterpart eight months later in the "October Revolution" of 1934, when Asturian miners, raising red and red-and-black flags over the mountain towns and cities of northern Spain, became the epicenter of a general uprising throughout the country. It was then that the increasingly well-known commander of the "Army of Africa," one Francisco Franco, brought Moorish troops as well as foreign legionnaires onto Spanish soil for the first time in five hundred years to defend "Christian Civilization" from "red barbarism." In a taste of the fierce counterrevolutionary retribution that was yet to come, two thousand miners were executed in the aftermath of the Asturias uprising and tens of thousands of Socialists, anarchosyndicalists, in smaller numbers Communists, and even some liberals found themselves in Spanish jails while the rest of the country smoldered in a savage class and regional hatred that found its full satisfaction two years later.

Under an ostensibly shared eagerness to free the October prisoners and in fear of growing rightist provocation of the kind that had finally brought the Viennese Socialists into insurrection, a "Popular Front" was slapped together from such widely disparate political groups as the Republican left, the Socialists, the Esquerra (Luis Companys's Catalan nationalists), the Communist Party, the Syndicalist Party (a political arm of the dissident anarchosyndicalist, Angel Pestaña), and the POUM (in Catalonia). The term "Popular Front" apparently originated in the French Communist Party and the Soviet-French Treaty of Mutual Assistance (May 1935) in which both countries vowed to aid each other if either was "threatened or in danger of aggression." With the Popular Front, all Western Communist Parties and all their front organizations made a sharp *volte face* from a previous totally insane policy of revolutionary adventurism, in which even the CNT was dubbed "reformist," to a queasy "line" of total accommodation to the "forces of democracy" and an abject surrender of all radical principles to reformism. That the new gospel of leftists joining with liberals was nothing less than Stalin's wholesale prostitution of the world's Communist Parties for "non-aggression" and preferably "mutual assistance" pacts between Russia and any power that was prepared to enter the Stalinist brothel became clear by 1936.

It is difficult today, when radical theory has retreated to the couloirs of the academy and radical practice to the smoke-filled rooms of liberal politicians, to recognize the crisis of conscience that "Popular Frontism" created in the Communist movement. Contrary to recent myths that the "Popular Front" was a welcome change of line, a waning generation from the era can still recall how American left-wing socialists taunted Communist Party members for the rapid desertion of their revolutionary ideals. In Spain, this took the form of the particularly cutting remark: "Vote Communist and Save Capitalism." The numbers who left "the Party" in bitterness were probably immense throughout the world. Yet neither "anti-fascism" nor a passion for "bourgeois democracy" can explain what kept thousands of revolutionary Communists in the Stalinist movement. That Communist parties were able to acquire more members in unprecedented numbers, many of whom were very tentative in their commitments, attests to the fact that even in the "red thirties," Western Europe and America contained more liberals than radicals. It also attests to the uncritical, often mindless loyalty of Communists to the Soviet Union as the "first Socialist country" in the world and to the legacy of the October Revolution — even as its leaders were being slaughtered en masse by Stalin's NKVD.

Equally fundamentally the "Popular Front" introduced a doctrinal crisis into the corpus of revolutionary Marxism. The very *raison d'être* for a Communist Party *anywhere* in the world had been Social Democracy's legacy of "betrayals," creating the need for a new revolutionary movement. "Betrayal," in the language of the day, meant the abandonment of Marx's basic, indeed unswerving strategy of revolutionary independence for all authentic "workers' parties." This precept, forcefully voiced by Marx and Engels in their famous "Address of the Central Committee to the Communist League" (March 1850), warned that "everywhere workers' candidates are put up alongside of the bourgeois-democratic candidates ... to preserve their independence." As if in anticipation of "popular frontism" a century later both men forbade Communists from allowing "themselves to be seduced by such arguments of the democrats as, for example, that by so doing they are splitting the democratic party and making it possible for the reactionaries to win."[5]

To abandon these precepts was to assail the authenticity of Communism as such, indeed, to discard the most fundamental principles of Bolshevism as a truly Marxist politics. It had been on the strength of these strategic ideas that the Bolshevik Party had come to power in 1917 and defined itself as a revolutionary movement. For Stalin in the Popular Front to adopt exactly what Marx Engels, and Lenin had regarded as the most "treacherous" features of "bourgeois democracy" and Social Democracy reduced world Communist movements to mere guardians of the Soviet Union and an extension of Stalinist foreign policy. If anything could justify so abject a role for Communists, it was their belief — held consciously or not — that Russia was the main force for the achievement of world socialism. This doctrinal mystification essentially replaced the power of the oppressed to *change* society and thereby *change themselves* in a supreme act of self-empowerment, with the power of a "workers' state" to instrumentally *redesign* society.

The logic of this mentality had disastrous ramifications, ones that exist today even as they did fifty years ago. This Popular Front mystification was to turn socialism from a *social* movement into a largely diplomatic one. World Communist Parties which had been spawned in a period of authentic revolution were to be denatured by the mythos of a socialism achieved by international power politics into mere tools for preserving or abetting the interests of a nation-state. The Popular Front, in effect, not only planted socialism in a geographical area and divested it of its ethical calling to redeem humanity; it rendered the "ideal," with all its visionary and critical meanings over the course of history, territorial and invested it with the fixity of the "real," notably as a mere instrument of national policy.*

The argument between the compromised Communist movement of the Popular Front and its leftist critics unfolded on a multitude of levels over the three tortured years that preceded the Stalin-Hitler pact of 1939. Left Socialists generally called it "class collaboration," with blunt clarity; the forfeiture of the very sense of revolutionary purpose that alone could defeat fascism, much less achieve socialism; the proclivity of liberals to deliver democratic liberties to fascists rather than yield power to

---

*Not surprisingly, Marx's "materialist conception of history" was also denatured, even its most simplistic forms. Once a theory that tried to explain social change as the product of far-reaching material forces, it increasingly explained change in terms of "conspiracies," an underlying theme of Stalin's purge trials in the 1930s. This mentality was not confined to Russia or to the 1930s: it has assumed gothic, indeed nightmarish proportions in the thinking of many self-proclaimed "radicals" who are far more entangled in the "cold war" than they are in Marxist theory. Accordingly, they see social change and social movements all too readily as "CIA conspiracies" if they contravene the interests of Russia and the so-called "socialist world." Such "explanations" were rampant in the 1950s when various Stalinists were obliged to explain the Hungarian Revolution, insurgent workers' movements in Eastern Europe generally, and more recently, the rise of Polish Solidarity. That the Miskito Indians in Nicaragua, to cite a particularly provocative example, have cultural and material concerns that stand at odds with those of the Sandinista government tends to be ignored, while their opposition to the Sandinista government is explained as a "CIA conspiracy," not as an indigenous people's movement with socially legitimate claims of its own. The "materialist conception of history" thus was the first victim of the belief that the "defense of the Soviet Union" is the defense of socialism as such. "Cold war socialism" is not only a nationalist diplomacy carried on in the theoretical guise of internationalism; it is a corruption of socialist theory to the level of espionage, the crude outcome of ideals placed in the service of a one nation and its foreign ministry.

an insurgent working class. Remote as the Popular Front era seems today, it is striking that leftist challenges to it have been supported by reality to an uncanny extent.

In Spain, the victory of the Popular Front in February 1936 virtually unleashed a revolution by itself. The organizations that orchestrated its electoral success allowed a government of liberal mice, marked by timidity and a fear of the working class and peasantry, to preside over their destiny. The incongruity between the bumbling Azaña regime in Madrid and the wave of strikes, rural land seizures, and gun-battles that swept over Spain between February and July, when Franco finally "pronounced" against the "Republic," is so stark and the logic of events that left only two choices by the summer of 1936 — either libertarian revolution or bloody authoritarian reaction — is so compelling that Franco's easy success in transporting the "Army of Africa" from Spanish Morocco to the mainland was an act of governmental betrayal in its own right.

The CNT placed all its militants on alert and blanketed Barcelona with workers patrols, but the other leftist parties which had formed the "Popular Front" were essentially quiescent. Even after Franco rose and the government attempted to strike a deal with the military, causing people to fill the streets demanding arms, the Communist and Socialist Parties jointly declared: "It is a difficult, not a desperate time. The government is sure it has adequate means to crush this criminal move. Should its means prove inadequate, the Republic has the Popular Front's solemn promise. It is ready to intervene in the struggle if it is asked to help. The government commands and the Popular Front obeys."[6]

It is not the case that no one knew early on that the army garrisons would rise — or, for that matter, when and where. Owing to its excellent intelligence service, which had penetrated the military, police, and security forces generally, the CNT had warned months in advance that the army was planning a coup in the summer of 1936 and that its base would be Spanish Morocco. Even more compelling, Colonel Escofet, the Republican police chief of Barcelona, had learned from informers and wiretaps that the rising would occur on July 19 at 5 A.M.,

To Remember Spain

exactly as the conspirators had originally planned, and he gave this information to the Catalan and Madrid governments. They met his information with disbelief — not because they regarded a coup as incredible but because they could not act upon the information without arming the people. That alternative was simply excluded. Indeed, as Escofet later frankly admitted, he blandly lied to CNT leaders who came to him demanding arms by "saying they could go home since the rising had been postponed."[7]

The very opposite, in fact, had happened: the rising was pushed forward by two days. As early as the morning of July 17, when Franco's aides broadcast news of the army rebellion, the naval station near Madrid intercepted the report and brought it to the Ministry of the Navy. The only decisive action the government took was to conceal it from the people — indeed, like Escofet, to lie by announcing the utterly false story that the uprising in Seville had been crushed. The lie was all the more horrendous because thousands of workers in the city were being systematically executed by the military after army rebels had vanquished them. It was only from popular initiative — first in Barcelona, where the army was defeated after two days of fighting by the combined action of the workers and sympathetic Civil Guards, and later in Madrid, Valencia, Málaga, and virtually all the major cities in central Spain — that coordinated resistance emerged from the political centers of the country.

There were no sensational victories by the army and no decisive failures by the people. Apart from the Andalusian cities which Franco and his generals quickly captured, as often by ruse as by arms, the *pronunciamiento* was essentially a military failure, and the conflict dragged on to its bloody conclusion for the greater part of three years. That Franco was able to establish himself on the mainland was due to the hesitation of the "Popular Front" regime which misled the people; partly because the leftist parties, fearful of challenging the government's authority, seemed to be sleepwalking through the opening days of the rebellion, and partly because this very government was negotiating with the military rather than arming the people. As a result, radical urban centers like Seville, Granada, and to the surprise of the army itself, Oviedo in Asturias and Saragossa in

Aragon, fell to local military commanders by sheer ruse because the workers had been kept in ignorance of what was happening elsewhere in Spain. The slaughter that occurred in all these cities when the army took over initiated a terrible hemorrhaging of the Spanish working class and peasantry, a bloodletting that turned Spain into a cemetery for more than thirty-five years. As Pierre Broué and Emile Témime conclude in their excellent account of the revolution and civil war, "In effect, each time that the workers' organizations allowed themselves to be paralyzed by their anxiety to respect Republican legality and each time their leaders were satisfied with what was said by the officers, the latter prevailed. On the other hand, the *Movimiento* of the generals] was repulsed where the workers had time to arm and whenever they set about the destruction of the Army as such, independently of their leaders' position or the attitude of 'legitimate' public authorities." [8]

There is nothing in this account that a revolutionary socialist or anarchist could not have predicted from the day the "Popular Front" came to power. The liberals played out their classical role with almost textbook exactness. The Socialist Party, divided between a cynical right and an irresolute left, was eaten away by indecision and a failure of nerve that brought its own conservative chieftains to the point of treachery. Finally, the anarchosyndicalist leaders, far less decisive than their rank-and-file militants, refused to take power in their Catalan stronghold as a matter of principle in the opening weeks of the revolution — only to compromise their most basic antistatist doctrines later by humbly entering the central government as ministerial fixtures. Harried by Communist and liberal assaults on the militia system and the collectivization, and by an increasingly deadly Stalinist terror, the CNT-FAI leadership withdrew into a posture of plaintive clients of the "Popular Front," whining rather than fighting against the rollback of the revolution that had been the result of a popular movement more than of their own efforts.

But what no one seems to have expected was the resoluteness with which the Spanish Communist Party played out its counterrevolutionary role, abetted by Soviet weapons,

"Comintern" agents, NKVD experts, and in no small part, individual members of the "International Brigades," who provided the PCE with some of its best assassins. The initial response of the Communists to Franco's *pronunciamiento* was designed to bolster the reputation of the liberal government which was trying to come to terms with the insurgent generals. More than any organization that professed to be "leftist," the PCE opened its doors to the most conservative elements that found themselves behind the "Republican" lines, becoming the rallying point for domestic reaction, and steadily ate away at the revolution in the name of "antifascism." Not only did it try to arrest collectivization, it tried to reverse it , restoring hierarchy in the institutions that formed the infrastructure of Spanish life and speaking openly for the bourgeois interest in Spanish society. The files of *Mundo Obrero*, the PCE's principal organ, are filled with journalistic declamations, manifestos, and editorials that denounce the militias in favor of a fully officered "Popular Army," lend support to the liberals and right-wing Socialists against criticism by the Socialist left and the anarchists, and denounce any exercise of power by the unions and revolutionary committees with the cry, "The slogan today is all power and authority to the People's Front government" (*Daily Worker*, September 11, 1936).

To explain why any self-professed radicals remained in the PCE is almost impossible without analyzing the organization's sense of priorities: the wishful identification of "socialism" on the part of its more committed members with a nation-state, even at the expense of a popular movement that was actively emancipatory elsewhere. In this very real sense, the Spanish Communist Party was no more Spanish than its Soviet counterpart and as a result of its identification of "communism" with Stalin's national policies, no more communist than the Catholic Basque movements that opposed Franco.

The "leftist" government formed by Largo Cabellero in September 1936 was aimed at mobilizing Socialist, anarchosyndicalist, and Communist leaders not only against the army but against the revolution initiated by their own rank-and-file. As Largo Caballero attested after he had been removed from office, Soviet intervention in Spanish affairs was brutally overt and demanding. The revolution was blemishing the Soviet Union's image as a respectable nation-state in the pursuit of diplomatic alliances. It had to be stopped. Caballero was anything but a revolutionary, but he had a real base in the Spanish Socialist Party which gave him enough freedom to act according to his own judgment, a fatal flaw in the eyes of the Communists.

Nevertheless it was under this regime that the revolution expired. On September 30, the "Popular Army" was proclaimed, to the delight of the liberals, Communists, and right-wing Socialists; indeed, nearly all parties and organizations on the left abetted the transformation of the militias into a conventional army. The distribution of weapons, equipment, and resources among different sectors of the front and to different regions of the country was scandalously governed by political considerations. They were even abandoned to Franco if the Communists and their allies suspected they would become available to the anarchosyndicalists. To cite one of many examples, Spain's only prewar cartridge factory in the "Republican" zone, at Toledo, was permitted to fall into the hands of Francoist forces rather than remove it to Barcelona which would have strengthened the revolutionary movement — this, despite pleas by José Tarradellas, the deputy of the Catalan premier Luis Companys, who personally visited Madrid to present his request for its removal. [9]

Reinforced by Soviet arms and the huge membership that it acquired largely from the middle classes, the PCE launched an outright assault on the collectives and the revolutionary committees, even purging the anarchosyndicalists, which *Pravda*, the organ of the Soviet Communist Party, declared "will be conducted with the same energy with which it was conducted in the U.S.S.R" (December 17, 1936). "Chekist organizations recently discovered in Madrid," warned the anarchosyndicalist newspaper *Solidaridad Obrera* on April 25, 1937, referring to NKVD-type secret prisons and police forces ". . . are directly linked with similar centers under a unified leadership and a preconceived plan of national scope." We do not have to go to George Orwell, a victim of these "Chekists" (the term applied to the Bolshevik secret police during the Russian Revolution), for personal verification of the charge. *Pravda* had already projected the formation of this network, and after the war, numerous anarchosyndicalists and POUMists gave detailed accounts of their own experiences at the hands of this Communist-controlled system of internal repression.

The decisive point in destroying the popular movement and reducing its militants to passivity came in early May 1937, when Catalan security forces under the personal command of the Communist commissioner of public safety, Salas, tried to seize the CNT-controlled telephone building in Barcelona. The attack triggered off a virtual insurrection by the Catalan working class, which had been nursing months of grievances against the Communists and liberals. Within hours, barricades were raised all over the city, and the "Lenin Barracks," the Communist military stronghold, was completely surrounded by armed workers. The insurrection spread beyond Barcelona to Lérida, where the Civil Guards surrendered their arms to the workers, to Tarragona, Gerona, and to militiamen on the Aragon front, who prepared to send detachments to the CNT urban centers. The dramatic five days between May 3 and 8, when CNT workers could have reclaimed their dwindling revolutionary conquests, were days not of defeat but of treachery — no less by the clique that led the CNT than the Communists, who were prepared to create a civil war within the civil war, irrespective of its toll on the struggle against the Francoists. Lacking even a modicum of this resoluteness, the "anarchist ministers," Montseny and García Oliver induced the CNT workers to lay down their arms and return to their homes. This self-inflicted defeat turned into an outright rout when superbly armed "Republican" assault guards entered Barcelona in force to contain its restive population. Barcelona had been turned from the center of the revolution into the cowed occupied zone of outright counterrevolution — at a cost in life, it may be noted, comparable to the losses the city had suffered in the army's uprising a year earlier.

The failure of the insurrection — the famous "May Days" — opened wide the gates of the Communist-led counterrevolution. Largo Caballero was forced to resign, replaced by Juan Negrín, who leaned heavily on PCE support up to the very end of the war. Two months later, the POUM was officially outlawed, and Andres Nín, its most gifted leader, murdered by Soviet agents in collusion with Thälmann Battalion members of the International Brigades. The anarchosyndicalists, too, suffered heavily, especially with the assassination of Carlo Bernieri, the authentic voice of Italian anarchism and a sharp critic of the CNT leadership. There is also compelling evidence that members of the Garibaldi Battalion of the International Brigades were implicated in his murder during the May Days. By August, the notorious Military Investigation Service (SIM) was formed under Negrín's premiership to intensify the Stalinist terror inflicted on militant anarchosyndicalists and POUM-ists. In the same month, the Moscow-trained thug Enrique Líster, led his Communist 11th Division into the last rural strongholds of anarchism, where he disbanded the Council of Aragon and an indeterminable number of collectives and cowed the revolutionary movement, under orders, by his own admission, to "shoot all the anarchists I had to."[10] The "Republican" government aimed the Belchite campaign, one of the bloodiest in the civil war," as much at demolishing the Council of Aragon, that anarchist state-within-the-state, as at achieving any significant results against the Nationalists," observes David Mitchell in his oral-history accounts of the civil war.[11]

Thereafter, the "Spanish war," as it was nonchalantly called by a bored world in the late 1930s, became nothing but a war — and a nightmare for the Spanish people. Army and people alike were now completely demoralized and "utterly pessimistic," observes Josep Costa, a CNT union leader who fought on the Aragon front. "The men were like lambs going to a slaughter. There was no longer an army, no longer anything. All the dynamic had been destroyed by the treachery of the Communist party in the May events. We went through the motions of fighting because there was an enemy in front of us. The trouble was that we had an enemy behind us too. I saw a comrade lying dead with a wound in the back of the neck that couldn't have been inflicted by the Nationalists. We were constantly urged to join the Communist party. If you didn't you were in trouble. Some men deserted to escape the bullying." That Communist execution squads were wandering over battlefields after the troops had pushed forward and were killing wounded anarchosyndicalists with their characteristic black-and-red insignia has also been told to me by CNT men who participated in the Battle of the Ebro, the last of the major "Republican" offensives in the civil war.

The end of the war on April 1, 1939, did not end the killings. Franco systematically slaughtered some 200,000 of his opponents between the time of his victory and the early 1940s in a carnage of genocidal proportions that was meant to physically uproot the living source of the revolution. No serious ideological efforts at conversion were made in the aftermath of the Francoist victory. Rather, it was a vindictive counterrevolution that had its only parallel, given the population and size of Spain, in Stalin's one-sided civil war against the Soviet people.

A revolutionary civil war of the kind that occurred in Spain is no longer possible, in my view, today — at least, not in the so-called "First World." Capitalism itself, as well as the classes that are said to oppose it, has changed significantly over the past fifty years. The Spanish workers were formed by a cultural clash in which a richly communal world, largely precapitalist, was brought into opposition to an industrial economy that had not yet pervaded the character structure of the Spanish people. Far from yielding a "backward" or "primitive" radical movement, these tensions between past and present created an enormously vital one in which the traditions of an older, more organic society heightened the critical perceptions and creative élan of a large worker-peasant population. The embourgeoisement of the present-day proletariat, not to speak of its loss of nerve in the face of a robotic and cybernetic technology, are merely evidence of the vastly changed social conditions and the overall commodification of society that has occurred since 1936.

Military technology, too, has changed. The weapons with which the Franco forces and the "Republicans" fought each other seem like toys today, when neutron bombs can be at the service of a completely ruthless ruling class. Force alone can no longer oppose force with any hope of revolutionary success. On this score, the greatest power lies with the rulers of society, not with the ruled. Only the hollowing out of the coercive institutions in the prevailing society, such as occurred in Portugal fairly recently and certainly in the Great French Revolution of two centuries ago — where the old society, divested of all support, collapsed at the first thrust — can yield radical social change. The barricade is a symbol, not a physical bulwark. To raise it denotes resolute intent at best — it is not a means to achieve change by insurrection. Perhaps the most lasting physical resistance the Spanish workers and peasants could have organized, even with Franco's military successes, would have been guerrilla warfare, a form of struggle whose very name and greatest traditions during modern times are Spanish. Yet none of the parties and organizations in the "Republican" zone seriously contemplated guerrilla warfare. Instead, conventional armies opposed conventional armies largely in trenches and as columns, until Franco's plodding strategy and overwhelming superiority of supplies swept his opponents from the field.

Could revolutionary warfare have defeated Franco? By this I mean a truly political war which sought to capture the hearts of the Spanish people, even that of the international working class, which exhibited a measure of class consciousness and solidarity that seems monumental by present-day standards. This presupposes the existence of working-class organizations that minimally would not have been a burden on the awakened people of Spain — and hopefully, would have contributed to the popular impetus. Given these conditions, my answer would be yes, as proved to be the case in Barcelona at the beginning, where Franco's army was defeated earlier than elsewhere. Franco's forces, which failed to gain victories in central Spain's major cities, could have been kept from taking such key radical centers as Seville, Córdoba, Oviedo, and Saragossa — the latter two of strategic importance, linking the most industrialized urban regions of Spain, the Basque country, and Catalonia. But the regime temporized with the aid of the "Popular Front" parties — particularly the Communists and right-wing Socialists — while confused workers in these key cities fell victim in almost every case to military ruses, not combat. With far greater determination than its enemies, the military drove a wedge between the Basques and Catalans that the "Popular Army" never overcame.

Even so, Franco's forces stalled significantly at various times in the war, such that Hitler expected his "crusade" to fail.[12]

The death blow to popular resistance was delivered by the Communist Party, which was willing to risk the collapse of the entire war effort in its program to dissolve the largely libertarian revolution — one which had tried, faintheartedly enough, to come to a modus vivendi with its opponents on the "left." But no such understanding was possible: the PCE sought to make the "Spanish war" respectable primarily in the Soviet Union's interests and to cloak itself for all the democratic world to see in the trappings of bourgeois virtue. The revolution had tarnished this image and challenged the explicitly counterrevolutionary function which the entire Communist International had adopted in the service of Soviet diplomacy. Hence not only did the Spanish Revolution have to be exterminated, its exterminators had to be seen as such. The "Reds" had to be regarded as a safe bet by London, Paris, and Washington — and they gradually were as the conflict in Spain came to an end.

By the time the war was internationalized by unstinting German and Italian aid to Franco and the Soviet Union's highly conditional and limited assistance to the "Republicans" — in exchange, I may add, for Spain's sizable gold reserves — revolutionary victory was impossible. The May Days could have produced a "Catalan Commune," a sparkling legacy on which the Spanish people could have nourished their hopes for future struggles. It might even have become an inspiration for radical movements throughout the world. But the CNT, already partly bureaucratized in 1936, became appallingly so by 1937, with the acquisition of buildings, funds, presses, and other material goodies. This reinforced and rigidified the top-down hierarchical structure that is endemic to syndicalist organization. With the May Days, the union's ministerial elite completely arrested the revolution and acted as an outright obstacle to its advance in later moments of crisis.

The Communist Party of Spain won all its demands for an army, decollectivization, the extermination of its most dangerous opponents, the Stalinization of the internal security forces, and the conversion of the social revolution into a "war against fascism" — and it lost the war completely. Soviet aid, selective and unreliable at best, came to an end in November 1938, nearly a half-year before Franco's victory, while Italian and German aid continued up to the end. When Stalin moved toward a pact with Hitler, he found the "Spanish war" an embarrassment and simply denied it further support. The "Western democracies" did nothing for "Republican" Spain despite that regime's success in suppressing internal revolution and its Western-oriented policy in international affairs. Thus, it denied Spanish Morocco, a major reservoir of Franco's troops, the independence that might have turned it against the rebel army, despite promises by Moroccan nationalists of support.

What was lost in Spain was the most magnificent proletariat that radical movements had ever seen either before or after 1936-39 — a classical working class in the finest socialist and anarchist sense of the term. It was a proletariat that was destroyed not by a growing material interest in bourgeois society but by physical extermination. This occurred largely amidst a conspiracy of silence by the international press in which the liberal establishment played no less a role than the Communist. It is appalling that Herbert M. Matthews, the *New York Times*'s principal correspondent on the so-called "Loyalist" side of the war, could write as recently as 1973, "I would say that there was a revolution of sorts, but it should not be exaggerated. In one basic sense, there was no revolution at all, since the republican government functioned much as it did before the war."[13] Whether this is stupidity or collusion with the forces that ended the "revolution of sorts," I shall leave for the reader to judge. But it was correspondents of this political temper who fed news of the "Spanish war" to the American people in the 1930s.

The literature that deals with the conflict, generally more forthright than what was available for years after the war, has grown enormously, supported by oral historians of considerable ability. Has the American left learned from these accounts or from the Spanish collectives, industrial as well as agricultural, which offer dramatic alternative models of revolutionary modernization to the conventional ones based on nationalized economies and centralized, often totalitarian, control? My answer would have to be a depressing no. The decline of the "New Left" and the emergence of a more "orthodox" one threatens to create a new myth of the "Popular Front" as a golden era of radicalism. One would suppose that the new material on Spain, largely left-wing in orientation, has been read by no one. The "Spanish war" is no longer cloaked in silence, but the facts are being layered over with a sweet sentimentality for the aging survivors of the "Lincoln Battalion" and the Mom-Pop stereotypes in films like *Seeing Red*.

The truth, indeed, is out — but the ears to hear it and the minds to learn from it seem to have been atrophied by a cultivated ignorance and a nearly total loss of critical insight. "Partyness" has replaced politics, mindless "loyalty" has replaced theory, "balance" in weighing the facts has replaced commitment, and an ecumenical "radicalism" that embraces Stalinists and reformists under the shredded banner of "unity" and "coalition" has replaced the integrity of ideas and practice. That the banner of "unity" and "coalition" became Spain's shroud and was used with impunity to destroy its revolution and risk delivering the country to Franco is as remote from the collective wisdom of the left today as it was fifty years ago in the cauldron of a bloody civil war.

Ultimately, the integrity of the Spanish left could be preserved only if it articulated the most deep-seated traditions of the Spanish people: their strong sense of community, their traditions of confederalism and local autonomy, and their profound mistrust of the state. Whether the American left shares with the Spanish left the popular legacy that the latter cleansed and rescued from the right is a crucial problem that cannot be discussed here. But insofar as the anarchists gave these traditions coherence and a radical thrust, converting them into a political *culture*, not merely a contrived "program," they survived generations of incredible persecution and repression. Indeed, only when the Socialists resolved the problem of the relationship between a political movement and a popular one by establishing their famous "houses of the people" or *casas del pueblo* in Spain's villages, neighborhoods, and cities did they become a vital movement in Spanish life and politics.

The "Popular Front" ruptured this relationship by replacing a popular culture with the "politics" of backroom "coalitions." The utterly disparate parties that entered into "coalitions" were united solely by their shared fear of the popular movement and of Franco. The left's need to deal with its own relationship to popular traditions which have a latent radical content — to cleanse these traditions and bring out their emancipatory aspirations — remains a legacy of the Spanish Civil War that has not been earnestly confronted, either by anarchists or by socialists. Until the need to form a political culture is clearly defined and given the centrality it deserves, the Spanish Revolution will remain not only one of the most inexplicable chapters of radical history but the conscience of the radical movement as a whole.

Notes

1. *The Spanish Civil War* (Part Five, "Inside the Revolution"), a six-part documentary produced by BBC-Granada, Ltd. This series is by far the best visual presentation of the Spanish Civil War I have seen and contains an enormous amount of original oral history. It is a primary source for material on the subject.

2. Ronald Fraser, "The Popular Experience of War and Revolution" in *Revolution and War in Spain, 1931-1939*, Paul Preston, ed. (London and New York, 1983), pp. 226-27. This book is another valuable source.

3. See Edward E. Malefakis, *Agrarian Reform and Peasant Revolution in Spain: Origins of the Civil War* (London and New Haven, 1970), pp. 284-92.

4. For an evaluation of the alternative approaches that Europe faced in the sixteenth century, including the *Comunero* revolt, see my *Urbanization Without Cities*. Manuel Castells's *The City and the Grassroots* (Berkeley and Los Angeles, 1983) contains a fascinating account of the revolt and its implications, in what I am inclined to believe is a departure from Castells's more traditional Marxist approach. For an English account of the *Comunero* revolt and a useful criticism of historical writing on the subject, see Stephan Haliczer's *The Comuneros of Castile* (Madison, 1981). For a general background on the relationship between Spanish anarchism and the popular culture of Spain, see my book *The Spanish Anarchists* (New York, 1976; AK Press, 1994).

5. Marx and Engels, *Selected Works*, vol. 1 (Moscow: Progress Publishers), p. 182.

6. Quoted in Pierre Broué and Emile Témime, *The Revolution and the Civil War in Spain* (Cambridge, 1972), pg. 100.

7. Quoted in David Mitchell, *The Spanish Civil War* (London and New York, 1982) p. 31. This book is based on the BBC-Granada television series, but just as the series does not contain a good deal of material in the book, so the book does not contain a good deal of material in the series. The interested reader is therefore well advised to consult both.

8. Broué and Témime, op. cit., p. 104.

9. See the interview with Tarradellas in Part Five of the BBC-Granada *Spanish Civil War* documentary.

10. Mitchell, op. cit., p. 156.

11. Ibid, p. 158-59. Although the motives behind the Belchite campaign verge on the incredible, they were not uncommon. Other cases of major conflicts — and crises — in the Spanish Civil War were motivated by similar political considerations, with no concern for the lives lost and the damage inflicted on the "coalition" against Franco.

12. Dénis Smyth, "Reflex Reaction: Germany and the Onset of the Spanish Civil War," in Preston, op. cit., p. 253.

13. Quoted in Burnett Bolloten, *The Spanish Revolution* (Chapel Hill, 1979), p. 59.

Also from AK Press

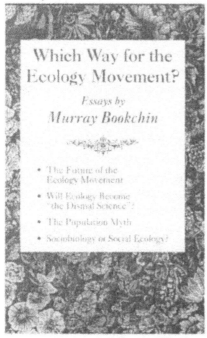

Which Way for the Ecology Movement?

Essays by Murray Bookchin

- The Future of the Ecology Movement
- Will Ecology Become "the Dismal Science"?
- The Population Myth
- Sociobiology or Social Ecology?

WHICH WAY FOR THE ECOLOGY MOVEMENT? by Murray Bookchin; ISBN 1 873176 26 0; 80pp two color cover, perfect bound 5-1/2 x 8-1/2; £4.50/$6.00. In the essays that make up this book, Murray Bookchin calls for a critical social standpoint that transcends both "biocentrism" and "ecocentrism"; for a new politics and ethics of complementarity, in which people, fighting for a free, nonhierarchical, and cooperative society, being to play a creative role in natural evolution. Bookchin attacks the misanthropic notions that the environmental crisis is caused mainly by overpopulation or humanity's genetic makeup. He resolutely points to the social and economic causes — patriarchy, racism, and a capitalistic "grow or die" economy as well as a hierarchical sensibility of dominating nature — as the problem the environmental movement must deal with. These ideas have to be confronted by environmentally concerned readers if the ecology movement is not to destroy its own potential as a force for social change and the achievement of a truly ecological society.

Murray Bookchin has been an essential, and prolific, author for over thirty years. All of his work currently in print is available mailorder from AK Press:

Ecology Of Freedom: The Emergence And Dissolution Of Hierarchy - $19.95/£11.99, paperback, Black Rose. A new revised edition of his magnus opus. The most systematic articulation of his ideas - his 'epistemology of liberation.'

The Philosophy Of Social Ecology - $18.95/£11.99, paperback, Black Rose. The latest set of essays on 'dialectical naturalism'.

Defending The Earth: A Dialogue Between Murray Bookchin and Dave Foreman - $10.00/£8.95, paperback, South End. Essays from their 'great debate.'

Post-Scarcity Anarchism - $18.95/£11.99, paperback, Black Rose. A seminal collection of essays on anarchism, ecology, appropriate technology and the anti-nuclear movement. Includes the classic 'Listen Marxist.'

Remaking Society: Pathways To A Green Future - $10.00/£8.95, paperback, South End. A primer on Bookchin's ideas, taking the reader through anthropology, the emergence of hierarchy and modern capitalism, technology, utopian radical solutions, urbanization and communities, and the ethics of social ecology.

The Limits Of The City - $17.95/£11.99, paperback, Black Rose. A history of city life which, once progressive, has reached its 'ultimate negation in the modern metropolis.'

The Modern Crisis - $9.95/£8.95, paperback, New Society. A primer of social ecology, and perhaps the most concise and approachable introduction to Bookchin's ideas.

Towards An Ecological Society - $18.95/£11.99, paperback, Black Rose. A classic collection of essays, including critiques of the environmental movement, explorations of the emancipatory possibilities for 'eco-communities and eco-technology', critiques of Marxism, and much more.

Urbanization Without Cities: The Rise And Decline Of Citizenship - $19.95/£11.99, paperback, Black Rose. The struggle for an environmentally oriented politics, a new ecological ethics and a citizenry that will restore the balance between city and country, humanity and nature.

Deep Ecology And Anarchism - $5.95/£2.50, paperback, Freedom. A debate (with Graham Purchase, Brian Morris and Rodney Aitchtey) on deep ecology, social ecology and anarchism.

Customers in Britain and Europe, please send your order to our UK address. Customers in North America or outside Europe, please send your order to our US address.

North America Ordering Information: please add $2 postage for the first title, and 50c for each subsequent title. For international orders, please add $4 for the first title, and 50c for each subsequent title. Payment must be made by check (drawn on a US bank), money order, or international money order made payable to AK Press in US dollars. Please send all orders to: AK Press, PO Box 40682, San Francisco, CA 94140-0682.

British and European Ordering Information: Postage for Britain and Europe is £1.00 for the first item, and 50p for each additional item. Payment must be made by check (drawn on a UK bank), money order, or international money order made out to AK Retail in Pounds Sterling. Please send all orders to: AK Press, 22 Lutton Place, Edinburgh, Scotland, EH8 9PE, Great Britain.

A new CD recording from AK Press

AK PRESS
AUDIO

NOAM CHOMSKY
THE CLINTON VISION

AK Audio, the newly formed audio imprint of AK Press, was created in order to bring the excitement and immediacy of the spoken word to people who care about politics. Reasonably priced, timely, and available on high-quality compact disc, **AK Audio** recordings deliver the best in political speech.

As an inaugural release, **AK Audio** makes Noam Chomsky, popular speaker, linguist, author, and political commentator, available to the home audience for the first time ever on compact disc.

In 1992 Bill Clinton was elected President of the United States. After 12 years of a Republican White House, voters hungry for change believed Clinton when he promised a new vision, a new activism, and a new direction for the US. In *The Clinton Vision*, Noam Chomsky speaks about the US President's actions on NAFTA, health care, crime, labor relations, foreign policy, and the economy.

"Chomsky has been unrelenting in his attacks on the American hierarchy. . . . [He] is up there with Thoreau and Emerson in the literature of rebellion."
—*Rolling Stone*

"If the job of a rebel is to tear down the old and prepare for the new, then this is Noam Chomsky, a 'rebel without a pause,' the 'Elvis of academia. . . .' As rock 'n roll in the 90s continues to be gagged, it is ironic that a man of 65 years turns out to be the real rebel spirit."
—*U2's Bono*

"How adroitly [Chomsky] cuts through the crap and actually says something."
— *Village Voice*

ISBN 1-873176-92-9 • $12.98/£11.99 • CD
• 56 minutes • two-color cover

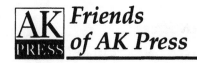

Friends
of AK Press

In the last 12 months, AK Press has published around 15 new titles. In the next 12 months we should be able to publish roughly the same, including new work by Murray Bookchin, Janet Biehl, Noam Chomsky, Jello Biafra, Stewart Home, a new anthology of situationist writings, new audio work from Noam Chomsky, new fiction from Kathy Acker, plus more. However, not only are we financially constrained as to what (and how much) we can publish, we already have a huge backlog of excellent material we would like to publish sooner, rather than later. If we had the money, we could easily publish 30 titles in the coming 12 months.

Projects currently being worked on include a collection of essays by Nestor Makhno; previously unpublished early anarchist writings by Victor Serge; more work from Noam Chomsky, Murray Bookchin and Stewart Home; Raoul Vaneigem on the surrealists; a new anthology of computer hacking and hacker culture; a Survival Research Laboratories book; the collected writings of Guy Aldred; a new anthology of cutting edge radical fiction and poetry; an updated version of the seminal anthology of contemporary anarchist writings *Re-Inventing Anarchy*; new work from Freddie Baer; Albert Meltzer's autobiography and an updated reprint of *The Floodgates of Anarchy*; the autobiography and political writings of former Black Panther and class war prisoner Lorenzo Kom'boa Ervin, and much, much more. As well as working on the new AK Press Audio series, we are also work-ing to set up a new pamphlet series, both to reprint long neglected classics and to present new material in a cheap, accessible format.

Friends of AK Press is a way in which you can directly help us try to realise many more such projects, much faster. Friends pay a minimum of $15/£10 per month into our AK Press account. All monies received go directly into our publishing. In return, Friends receive (for the duration of their membership), automatically, as and when they appear, one copy *free* of *every* new AK Press title. Secondly, they are also entitled to 10 percent discount on *everything* featured in the current AK Distribution mail-order catalog (upwards of 3,000 titles), on *any* and *every* order. **Friends**, if they wish, can be acknow-ledged as a **Friend** in all new AK Press titles.

To find out more on how to contribute to *Friends of AK Press*, and for a Friends order form, please do write to:

AK Press
PO Box 40682
San Francisco, CA 94140-0682

AK Press
22 Lutton Place
Edinburgh, Scotland EH8 9PE

Some Recent Titles from AK Press

TELEVISIONARIES: THE RED ARMY FACTION STORY 1963 TO 1993 by Tom Vague; ISBN 1 873176 47 3; 112pp two color cover; perfect bound 5-1/2 x 8-1/2; £4.50/$6.95. An irreverent chronological history and analysis of the terrorist group that have shot and bombed their way through the last three decades. From student radicalism to Stammheim to Euroterrorism, this is the only book in print which charts the raise and raise of the armed guerilla group that launched 1,000 t-shirts.

TESTCARD F: TELEVISION, MYTHINFORMATION AND SOCIAL CONTROL constructed by Anonymous; ISBN 1 873176 91 0; 80 pp four color cover, perfect bound 5-1/2 x 8-1/2; £4.50/$6.00. Using savage image-text cut and paste, this book explodes all previous media theory and riots through the Global Village, looting the ideological supermarket of all its products.

END TIME: NOTES ON THE APOCALYPSE by G.A. Matiasz; ISBN 1873176 96 1; 320 pp four color cover, perfect bound 5-1/2 x 8-1/2; £5.95/$7.00. A first novel by G.A. Matiasz, an original voice of slashing, thought provoking style. "A compulsively readable thriller combined with a very smart meditation on the near-future of anarchism, *End Time* proves once again that science fiction is our only literature of ideas." — Hakim Bey

ECSTATIC INCISIONS: THE COLLAGES OF FREDDIE BAER by Freddie Baer, preface by Peter Lamborn Wilson; ISBN 1 873176 60 0; 80 pages, a three color cover, perfect bound 8 1/2 x 11; £7.95/$11.95. This is Freddie Baer's first collection of collage work; over the last decade her illustrations have appeared on numerous magazine covers, posters, t-shirts, and album sleeves. Includes collaborations with Hakim Bey, T. Fulano, Jason Keehn, and David Watson.

STEALWORKS: THE GRAPHIC DETAILS OF JOHN YATES by John Yates; ISBN 1 873176 51 1; 136 pp two color cover, perfect bound 8-1/2 x 11; £7.95/$11.95. A collection to date of work created by a visual mechanic and graphic surgeon. His work is a mixture of bold visuals, minimalist to-the-point social commentary, involves the manipulation and reinterpretation of culture's media imagery.

AK Press publishes and distributes a wide variety of radical literature. For our latest catalog featuring these and several thousand other titles, please send a large self-addressed, stamped envelope to:

AK Press
22 Lutton Place
Edinburgh, Scotland
EH8 9PE, Great Britain

AK Press
P.O. Box 40682
San Francisco, CA
94140-0682

CPSIA information can be obtained
at www.ICGtesting.com
Printed in the USA
JSHW050158100722
27671JS00002B/10